GRANDPARENTING

GRANDPARENTING

A guide for today's Grandparents with over 50 activities to strengthen one of life's most powerful and rewarding bonds

SHARON
WEGSCHEIDER-CRUSE

ILLUSTRATED BY
BEATRICE BENJAMIN

Science & Behavior Books
Palo Alto, California

Other Science & Behavior Books by Sharon Wegscheider-Cruse

Another Chance: Hope and Health for the Alcoholic Family
Experiential Therapy for Co-Dependency: A Manual
Family Reconstruction: The Living Theater Model
Learning to Know Yourself Workbook

Science & Behavior Books by Virginia Satir

New Peoplemaking
Conjoint Family Therapy, 3rd ed.

All above titles available from:
Science & Behavior Books
Post Office Box 60519
Palo Alto, CA 94306
1 (800) 547-9982
FAX: (415) 965-8998

Additional Books by Sharon Wegscheider Cruse

Choicemaking
Learning to Love Yourself
Coupleship
The Miracle of Recovery
Understanding Co-Dependency
Life After Divorce

The above titles are available from:
Health Communications, Inc.
3201 S.W. 15th Street
Deerfield Beach, FL 33442
1(800) 851-9100

The Family Trap
Intimacy and Sexuality

The above titles are available from:
Onsite Training and Consulting at Sierra-Tucson
16500 N. Lago del Oro Parkway
Tucson, AZ 95737
1(800) 341-7432

Printed in the United States of America

Library of Congress Catalog Card Number 95-68095

ISBN 0-8314-0085-4

Edited by Amy Wilner
Illustrations by B. Benjamin
Book design by Joel Friedlander
Printed and bound by Haddon Craftsmen

To my five wonderful grandchildren,
Matthew, Melanie, Christopher, Ryan, & Cheyenne,
and any more to come,
and to my daughters, Sandra and Deborah,
who brought them into the world —
each of you holds a special place in my heart.

And to my husband Joe —
I could not be the kind of grandmother I am
if he were not the grandfather he is.

Acknowledgements

I would like to acknowledge my editor, Amy Wilner, for having both the child's interest and my own at heart, and for continually simplifying complex concepts. It has been a joy to work with her. David Spitzer, of Science & Behavior Books, has been there for me the entire time with this project, and I thank him for his enthusiasm, his interest, and his curiosity throughout.

A very special thank you goes to Uncle Pat, Uncle Phil, Aunt Carla, and Aunt Sue, who have demonstrated in so many ways that when it comes to bringing care and joy and nurturance to young people, anyone, not just grandparents, can be grand.

Contents

Acknowledgements vi

Introduction 1

The Influential Link:
The Many Roles of Today's Grandparents 13

Meeting Special Challenges 47

Activities 81

    Bonding with New Grandchildren 88

    Growing with a Pre-School or School-Age Grandchild 96

    Staying Close with Older Grandchildren 128

    Young Adults 140

    The Family History Project 143

Resources for Grandparents 163

About the Author 168

Introduction

"The entry of a child into any situation
changes the whole situation."

— IRIS MURDOCH

Before I became a grandparent, I had been a wife, a mother, a successful professional, a public speaker, and somewhat of a public figure. My life had been rich and exciting. But when I saw some of my friends become totally consumed by something their grandchild said or did, I couldn't relate. I couldn't understand how these people could be so involved with their grandchildren, and I imagined it was only because they had so little else going on in their lives. Although being a mother has been my biggest challenge and my greatest fulfillment, I still didn't understand all this fuss about grandbabies.

And a few years ago, when I was making out my will, my lawyer asked what sort of arrangements I wanted to make for my grandchildren. I was surprised. I told him I didn't have any grandchildren yet, and that I would like to provide as best I could for my children and trust that whatever they wanted to do for their own children would be best. I said I couldn't see myself becoming so attached to my future grandchildren that I would ever be in a position to make such important decisions for them. Needless to say I did this all with a very rational mind, full of clear thinking...

And then something changed. I believe it took all of five minutes for that change to occur, maybe less. It happened on a beautiful October morning when I was sitting in a hospital waiting room in Minneapolis with only a wall between myself and my youngest daughter, who was giving birth to her first child. I could hear my daughter through those very thin walls, and though her husband was the one holding her hand and helping her through the process, I felt totally bonded to her. Then I heard the cry of new life, the same sound people have heard through the ages as a new child makes its way into the world, only this one belonged to my first grandchild.

When I heard this sound I felt very deeply connected — to my own father, who had been dead for many, many years, and to my mother, who had been gone just a few years. I felt connected to my grandmother, who taught me so much and provided such a safe place for me to grow up. I even felt connected to my great grandmother, whom I never got to know personally, but whose name was given to me. In that moment it was as if the world had stopped, and there was nothing more real than the arrival of this wonderful child, and all of the powerful emotions the event evoked. At the time, I didn't yet know if it was a boy or a girl, but I knew, in the midst of feeling close to all of those who had come before me, that this was a child to whom I would feel deeply connected forever. And though I would not have anticipated it, indeed, had not anticipated it, my life changed as profoundly in that moment as it had changed three times before when I had given birth to my own children.

In just a few short minutes I was right there in the birthing room, and I had the opportunity to hold my grandson in my arms, and to feel a part of the entire life process in a new and wondrous way.

My daughter's cries of pain had ended, and she was glowing and beautiful in her bed. She was still my own little girl, my youngest child, and my heart swelled with love for her as well as for my grandson. She had just become a mother, and I knew we had even more to share with each other than we had had before. I also felt great love for my son-in-law, and for the love he had for my daughter and their child.

I was able to go to their house and spend a few days watching my daughter as she began her mothering, watching her husband as he began his fathering, and bonding with my new grandson. It was a glorious time, and I was very tired and happy when I returned to my own home in Nevada. I had been in the house only hours when we received a phone call that my other daughter had just gone into labor in Minnesota, and wanted me there with her in the delivery room. I immediately raced back to the airport and began the journey by air and car that would bring me to her. In a few hours I was in her birthing room where, for the first time, I actually witnessed the birth of a child (my own childrens' births had occurred under partial anesthesia). Through this experience I understood so much more clearly what had taken place just days earlier with the birth of my grandson. I held my tiny granddaughter in my arms after watching her being born, after feeling the pain and excitement with my daughter, and now I felt very rich indeed.

Even with all of this, I couldn't fathom how important "grandparenting" was going to become to me. Since that week, I've been given two more grandsons and another granddaughter, and these five young people fill my life in the most amazing way.

Now, grandparenting is a markedly varied experience. Some grandparents have the opportunity to be physically close to their children and grandchildren. Others are separated by geographic distance. I have had both experiences, and can honestly say that I wish I could live close enough to all my grandchildren to be a part of their daily lives. Physical proximity is not, however, the only factor that determines what kind of grandparent you may be.

For myself, I realized that in every other area of my life which had become important to me over time, I made a tremendous effort to build and sustain. I've done this with my career, and with personal relationships. For example, having a life partner and soul mate holds great value for me. So I've made commitments again and again to keep my primary relationship a very high priority. Many years ago I attended a seminar where I was told that we know where our values are if we pay attention to where we spend our time, our energy, and our money. (In this context and throughout this book, it's crucial to understand that money is "spent" relatively — no relationship costs a particular amount, and, ideally, we spend according to our means.) I know for a fact that my partnership has required a great deal in these areas. My husband and I have both had very fast-paced careers involving lots of travel and pulls from many directions. There were plenty of times when our work and lifestyles could have pulled us apart. We had to make difficult decisions to remember that our relationship was of such importance and value that certain other things had to be sacrificed instead. But the rewards have been incredible.

My children have been another unspeakably valuable part of my life. Today they are among my closest friends, and I think I can say with confidence that I am a good friend to them. Just because I gave birth to these people doesn't give me the right to demand their love or attention. As adults, we have relationships that are as good as we create for ourselves and each other. Again, this means spending our time, our energy, and even, to the extent each has been able, our money. We have spent vacations together and made a priority of attending family gatherings, even when there were conflicts with other interests. We have worked hard to maintain our friendships with each other. And the truth is that we are growing closer the older we get. As this happens, we don't have to work quite so hard because we genuinely share so many of the same interests, but there were many years when this wasn't the case, and different ideas and values could have pulled us apart. The fact that we didn't drift in this way is only because we made decisions not to, and we made choices to accord with those decisions. These days, I'm aware that it's going to take the same kind of energy, focus, time, and money that I've put towards my partnership and towards my relationships with my children to create good, rich relationships with my grandchildren.

My own grandmother had a wonderful outlook on relationships:

> People are like flowers. Some are like dandelions, some are roses, some are lilies, some are mums, and some are orchids. Some are fragile, some are strong, some need lots of attention, and some do best with no attention. But if we are to have the most beautiful gardens and the most beautiful bouquets, we need some of each. We have to learn what to water and how often, and also when not to water. To truly love flowers, we have to get to know them individually, and treat them accordingly.

I often think of my grandmother as I realize that each of my grandchildren is different, and that I'll have to work to get to know each of them fully. I have made the decision to have relationships with each of them as individuals — I don't want to group them together as "the grandchildren." I want them to be Matthew, Melanie, Christopher, Ryan, and Cheyenne. This means I'm going to have to know who each of them is, and what happens in each of their lives in order to be able to ask them questions specific to their days and interests and friends and joys and sorrows, to be able to provide them with experiences that are appropriate and rewarding based on a real understanding of who they are as individuals. Wanting us to be a rich part of each other's lives means committing to an investment in time and energy.

Now, for many of us, our children's families may not look very much like those we grew up in, or like the one we provided for them as they were growing up. It may be that our grandchildren are growing up in a single-parent home, or in one with two mommies or two daddies. Our grandchildren may be adopted, or have siblings who are. They may have step- or half-siblings as a result of divorce and re-marriage. Their parents may have different religious, racial, or ethnic backgrounds. The careful choices or less controlled circumstances that make the family lives of our children and grandchildren very different from our own can evoke complex and sometimes painful feelings. Whatever the case, it is important to remember that our grandchildren are innocent, and that they deserve our love and respect regardless. They also deserve as much healthy, loving interaction and as many models for good relationships around them as possible. As a family therapist with decades of experience, I've seen time and again that shared love for a child can promote the healing of past wounds between the child's parents and grandparents. A grandchild can also provide a catalyst or inspiration for getting closer to our children's spouses or partners.

Grandparenting holds great joys. It also comes with responsibilities, and, inevitably, as with any familial relationship, there are challenges. In good times and in trying times, all of these elements are present. They may even all be present in a single moment! The important thing to remember is that grandparents are unique in a child's life, and so, irreplaceable. To be the parent of a child's parent means you can bring something to that child no one else can give, a love and understanding and attachment and caring that comes from the connectedness of generations. Some of us wonder how to show all that we feel, and what exactly it is we have to give our grandchildren. The answer is anything but one-dimensional. In the first section of this book, I discuss the many roles a grandparent can play in a child's life, and address the important keys to establishing and maintaining a healthy, close relationship with your grandchildren. However joyous the love between a grandchild and grandparent can be, life presents challenges to us all. The second section focuses on ways a grandparent can help a grandchild through some of these very real difficulties. Finally, the third section of the book presents ideas for all kinds of activities grandparents and grandchildren can share, from arts and crafts to traveling together, from telephone calls to games, from correspondence to hikes and picnics, from playing post office to using computers.

It's only in recent years — and perhaps as a result of so many working parents having less time to spend with their children — that writers, counselors, and families have begun to focus on the role of grandparents, and have begun to come to terms with the influential link that exists between grandparent and grandchild. The next few years should be a rich and fertile time for developing some clearer guidelines for maximizing this connection.

Meanwhile, accept each grandchild in your life as a unique blessing. Know that you have much to offer this child, and accept the love you get in return as a gift of grace and beauty. Remember that your time and energy are the most valuable things you have to offer. Give these enthusiastically, and you'll be amazed at the rewards.

A Note About Grandfathers

My life has been blessed by being able to share my grandparenting with a loving husband who thrills at being a grandfather. As I wrote this book, I naturally offered my thoughts, feelings and experiences from a Grandma's point of view. Yet everything I say about grandparenting, or even about being a grandmother, equally applies to being a grandfather.

My husband, "Grandpa Joe," as he's sometimes referred to in these pages, has added many insights and experiences to this volume. Some of these are explicitly attributed to him, others are simply woven into the text.

Grandmothers and grandfathers alike are welcomed to these pages as they are welcomed into the lives of little children — with open arms, and a ready heart.

"Gentleness is not a quality exclusive to women."

— Helen Reddy

The Influential Link:

The Many Roles of Today's Grandparents

"To be told we are loved is not enough. We must feel loved."

— MARCIA JACOBER

In my 25 years as a family therapist, it has always been my practice to see as many of the family members as possible when doing family and/or marriage counseling. We may express our concerns about just one person or we may focus on a very particular situation, yet a closer exploration usually takes us into the dynamics or workings of a whole family system.

Not only have I sat in countless family counseling sessions, including plenty with three generations present, I've also had a key role in developing a process known as "psychodrama," which allows families to role-play their family dynamics with the help of people who aren't their real relatives. This process gives people an opportunity to "confront" members of their family systems in a safe way, even if the actual family members are physically or emotionally absent, or deceased. (For more information about the psychodrama process, see Wegscheider-Cruse, Higby, Klontz & Rainey, *Family Reconstruction: The Living Theater Model.* Palo Alto, CA: Science &

Behavior Books, 1995). In many, many instances, it turned out that the relative someone felt closest to as a child, the one he or she felt safest with, and most loved by, was a grandparent.

Of my own four grandparents, one died before I was born, one was distant and unavailable to me, one died when I was 12 years old, and one was very present for me until she died when I was 34 years old. This was Grandma Olson.

Grandma Olson loved me openly and unconditionally. She regularly asked me how I felt and what I was thinking. She laughed with me all the time, and we had lots of secrets we shared only with each other. She was generously affectionate and loving, giving lots of hugs and kisses whenever I wanted them (see the section below on the ABCs of Trust for more about physical affection between grandparents and grandchildren). We had tremendous amounts of fun together, some of which came from doing things we weren't "supposed to do," but which were ultimately harmless and gave us a shared sense of adventure, like sneaking bologna sandwiches onto our many train rides and enjoying them instead of going to the dining car, giggling when we were supposed to be serious (sometimes even in church!), wearing unconventional clothes...

I know that much of the security I have felt as an adult came from the security I experienced being the grandchild of someone as loving as Grandma Olson. And I have always believed that if I could be a grandmother like the one she was, I might be able to pass on to my grandchildren the amazing gift of unconditional love, which may be at the heart of emotional security.

In fact, for many people, the seeds of self-acceptance are planted by a grandparent. This occurs at a very primary level, that is, before words or even thought, at the level of *feeling*. The person who helps you develop your self-acceptance is forever special in your life, forever profoundly important. When you're lucky enough to be able to build on this connection, this "influential link," and maximize the potential for love, safety, and joy, it is one of the most satisfying relationships there is.

*   *   *

In all species there seems to be the desire to protect and care for the young. The love between lion and cub, dog and puppy, elder elephants and the babies of the herd... Because humans have the particular thought processes that we do, including memories, expectations, and the ability to look backwards and forwards, this love between parent and child is intensified and sophisticated. When that love extends one more generation, it can be incredibly expansive.

As a grandparent makes a deep connection with a grandchild, their bond tends to be "pure," that is, unfettered or un-bothered by the responsibility, constancy, and need to educate that permeate the parent-child relationship. In most cases, the hard work of child-rearing is the rightful responsibility of the parent, and children are entrusted to their parents for their growth and development. Grandparents have usually long since completed their work in this capacity with their own children. Now their role is simply to be "extra" — extra love, nurturing, and support.

Another freedom inherent in the grandparent-grandchild relationship is that neither feels a need to prove anything. Grandparents are often past the busiest stage of their working lives, and don't feel the same drive towards accomplishment as many working parents do. They are also usually old enough to feel free of the social burden of having to prove themselves personally. Young grandchildren are similar in that they are without baggage — they are new to the world, and unencumbered by responsibilities and worries. As children get older, of course, they begin to take on concerns and to face very real problems, but these are usually worked on and worked through with parents. The relationship between a grandparent and a grandchild has a kind of roominess to it, a feeling of spaciousness that comes from not having to deal with daily concerns, from not living together constantly, and, in most cases, from each person being in one of the more carefree phases of life.

This is not to say that there aren't some conflictual or problematic aspects to the influential link. Let's explore the whole picture....

Positive Aspects of the Influential Link

Throughout my work in the field of psychology and counseling, my observation has been that the link between grandparents and grandchildren is second in importance only to that between parent and child. The amazing thing is that it would seem this link remains constant throughout life — from the wonderful infancy and toddler years throughout childhood and adolescence and well into adulthood. When I was in my 30s and she was in her 70s, my grandmother and I used to sit in front of the fire at my house, have a cup of coffee or a glass of wine and just visit, like old friends. I loved her vitality.

Now, I had a very young grandmother, only about forty years older than me. And some grandparents are certainly much older than their grandchildren, which will, inevitably, shorten the amount of time they're going to have together. But vitality is something that may not have anything to do with age. And the vitality of the connection between grandparent and grandchild is the same.

Some grandparents feel distant to young children, part of an unimaginable generation. They may move slowly, and it can be difficult to connect either verbally or emotionally. There doesn't seem to be anything in common except the accident of being related. It's just hard to feel close.

Then there's the active, interested, and interesting grandparent. This person can be young or old in years, may have snow-white hair and tons of wrinkles, or look young enough to be the child's parent instead of grandparent. What sets this grandparent apart is his or her interest in current times, sense of humor, and energetic approach to life. And while some may have a physically active lifestyle, even a grandparent who is physically impaired can possess the qualities of intellectual, emotional, and personal vitality.

Grandparents who make a commitment to a lifetime of interests and growth present a very different picture to their families than do the stereotypes of the grandfather who does nothing but sit in his chair reading and the grandmother who does nothing but stay in the kitchen.

All older people have choices about how to approach life, and about what kind of grandparents we want to be. Among the many wonderful, positive roles we can take in our grandchildren's lives are those of nurturer, family historian, mentor and teacher, student, caretaker, and magician.

Nurturer. This role is the easiest to take, and one which comes naturally to most grandparents. Providing grandchildren with unconditional love and acceptance is hard for most grandparents to resist! But what does it look like?

"Social security" is a concept with which many grandparents are familiar. And although in today's world social security is a complex socioeconomic reality, the original idea behind it was to offer older people a kind of cushion in order to alleviate undue financial hardship. I would like to suggest that there is a kind of *emotional* social security, that is, an emotional cushion, which children need and deserve much the same as older people need and deserve a financial one. I also believe that this cushion is something grandparents can provide.

Let me try to explain what I mean through examples.

One winter it seemed as though one of my grandsons was going through a hard time. No matter where he turned around, he would fall down and get up with a cut or bruise. Three times that winter he ended up in the emergency room getting stitches. After one of these visits he called me on the phone and said, "Grandma, I just had to go to the hospital and have some more stitches." I asked him about what had happened, and about what it was like to see the doctor, and he told me. Then he said, "Whenever I feel sad, or whenever I'm crying or I get afraid, I want to call you and tell you about it, Grandma." I can't explain how good that made me feel. My daughter got on the phone and said, "Whenever Matthew seems to be scared or hurt, he wants to call you."

We can provide our grandchildren with a sense of security by providing a consistently available "safe space" for them, and for their feelings. We can become one of their most dependable sources of sympathy and understanding.

I remember traveling with my granddaughter Melanie, staying in a motel, and accidentally leaving behind her special pink blanket. We didn't discover it was missing until we were already on the airplane headed home. Now there were lots of ways to handle the situation. First of all, the blanket was inexpensive, so I immediately went out and bought another, and was preparing to give it to her when I realized how sad she was at not having her *special* blanket — the one that had accompanied her to Disney World, that had been held over her head during the scary parts of "Beauty and the Beast," that had been her friend It became quite clear that she needed *this* blanket. My husband and I both called the motel in Florida where we had left it, and explained the significance of the blanket. Fortunately, the motel catered to a lot of families with small children and the manager understood the importance of such a thing. They put a tracer on their laundry because the blanket had not been found in the room, and sure enough, they found it. Now, instead of simply having the motel send the blanket directly to her at her house, I wanted to let her know how important it was to me that she and her blanket be reunited. I called my daughter and had her explain to

Melanie that Grandma cared very much about her missing blanket, and had done everything she could to find it for her, and that it would be coming in the mail. So not only did she get her blanket, she also knew that I appreciated what it meant to her, how much I cared about what she cared about. Perhaps as our grandchildren move through their lives and confront moments of sadness and loss and fear, we can let them know that they can count on us to really listen, and to really care.

Another grandson, Christopher, and I often sit in the back seat of his parents van when we drive around together as a family. On one of these trips with his family, Christopher was cranky and tired, altogether out of sorts. He'd had a bit of a tantrum, his parents had verbally disciplined him, and now he was crying quietly. I didn't want to contradict anything his parents had said or done, so I remained silent as he continued to cry quietly in his car seat over the next mile or so. Finally, in the dark, I simply reached out and took his tiny hand in mine. We traveled several more miles to get home, during which neither he nor I said anything. As we pulled into the parking lot, he held tight to my hand and said, "I love you, Grandma." I could feel his quiet comfort, and his peace. I knew he was feeing secure and safe. Maybe this is part of what grandparents are for.

Simply put, there are times when a child's parents aren't available, emotionally, physically, financially, or otherwise, and grandparents are. With older children, it can be nice to give them a card with your phone number on it, and teach them how to call collect. Make sure you inform the children's parents and get permission, of course.

Being available to your grandchildren can be a gift to everyone, including the children's parents. Which leads me to another point.

During my own active years of parenting, I had some real difficulties. Finances were extremely tight, and, as a single parent struggling to continue my education, so was time. Once my kids were grown, I spoke with one of my daughters about those days, and asked if there was any way that now, in my older years, I could make up for some of the lost time and the experiences we had missed.

"Maybe," she answered, "you can be there for my children."

She was right. We can have new experiences through grandparenting, many of which can also heal us and others whom we love.

Not all grandparents can offer to "be there," but many can and do. This can involve physical, emotional, or financial security in any combination. Grandparents who actually act as parents are discussed in the section on Meeting Special Challenges. Financial assistance is not always possible, and, again, any expenditure of money mentioned in this book should be understood to be relative — we each spend according to our means. Certainly if you are fortunate enough to be able to offer this assistance, it should be appreciated. But it is likely that the most meaningful gift to your grandchild will always be the emotional connection and security you can provide. This goes hand-in-glove with establishing and maintaining a trusting relationship with your grandchild; together this security and trust are the basis for all of the other ways of being in your grandchild's life that are discussed in further detail below.

As children become teenagers, a sometimes fragile balance needs to be maintained. These are the years when parent-child relationships can become strained, to say the least. It's important for everyone involved to know that grandparents can be additional sources of listening, advice, comfort, nurturing, security, etc. The delicacy of the situation comes in managing to be present, but not attempting to substitute for parents or act as a wedge between parent and child.

Family historian. My home is filled with items which are priceless to me — afghans and quilts made by my mother, a music box and piano owned by my grandmother, wall hangings made by an aunt, photographs framed by my son, a favorite lamp of my father's, art work made by my children and grandchildren, and 26 albums filled with photographs recording all the important events of my family....

My children and grandchildren love to see these things which tell stories and provide a sense of connection to their own histories when they visit me. As time goes on, I plan to share all of these treasured possessions with the family so that they can have some of this history in their own homes as well. In the albums, I've collected as many family stories as I could, and have added them to the pictures. To date, my grandchildren can look backwards and be introduced to five generations of pictures and stories! There is also much history to be passed on orally: the fire that destroyed Grandpa's business; the 1961 snowstorm when all the airports closed and no one got home for Christmas; the match that was dropped into the 4th of July fireworks and caused one giant explosion; Grandma graduating from college in her late 30s; Great-Grandpa's suicide during a depression; Great-Grandma's devotion to music; how the family farm got passed down to Dad... the list goes on and on.

> *Remember, the primary bond is always between the parent and the child. The "extras" between a grandparent and grandchild are a bonus.*

Such stories and heirlooms, such history, help any grandchild to feel a genuine connection to the people who came before. If enough is shared, the child can come to "know" the personality, essence, or character of these people, even if they never get to meet them. And it may just be that the hunger we are all born with for characters, the hunger that is satisfied by fairy tales and story books and cartoons and movies, that all of this is also alive for us with respect to the people in our own families as well.

(The Family History Project at the end of the Activities section invites you to begin the rich and joyous experience of this sharing with your grandchild.)

Mentor and Teacher. Someone once told me that we need both mentors and teachers in our lives — sometimes the two are found in the same person. Mentors support us, and teachers challenge us. Both take us beyond wherever we currently are. Grandparenting is the perfect opportunity to share our special skills and talents (more on this idea is offered in the Activities section). We all have them, we simply need to recognize them, and share them.

From my own grandmother, for example, I learned *acceptance of all people* — she used to say to me, "Always remember you are no better than anyone else, but always just as good"; *love of cooking* — there was something comforting and loving about walking into her house or apartment and smelling the wonderful aromas of home-made doughnuts, apple pie, vegetable soup, or roast beef, and I grew up wanting to do that for others; *true spirituality* — my grandmother believed in loving and caring for all people, regardless of their position in life, their race, their economic status, disability, or age, and she taught me to meet people and see their souls; and *joy* — my grandmother loved to have an ice cream cone before dinner, be the last one home from the dance, open a few presents before Christmas Day, laugh and giggle... she could always find the best in everyone, and enjoy it, and I have tried to pass on this love for life to my grandchildren (Melanie looked up at me once and said, "I like your laugh, Grandma, it makes me laugh too.)"

Role Model. I had many wonderful role models, including not just my grandmother but some aunts and uncles. Because of the importance of family that was displayed through everyone's commitment to family visits and involvement in each other's lives, I always knew I was special just because I existed as part of this group of people who were related to each other. This produced a profound sense of belonging and self-worth for me. My own family model demonstrated that generations could blend well together, and that we could all learn from each other. Because of the Depression and World War II, both my mother and grandmother had needed to work to help care for their families. Later in my life as a single parent, I appreciated having had these models for being a working mother and taking care of myself and my family. And now, as I get older, I've made a commitment to care for my health and pursue an active lifestyle. I hope that the way I age may offer a positive role model for my grandchildren. Whether in career, hobbies, attitudes, or values, grandparents have a great opportunity and responsibility to be the best role models they can be.

Student. As children grow, they need to learn leadership abilities. For this, they need places to practice. Grandparents can provide such a place. As a grandchild learns about a topic of interest, current and future technologies, better eating habits and nutrition, dances, music, investments, etc., he or she has an opportunity to teach grandparents who are willing to learn. In this situation, everyone comes out ahead. And while being a teacher can enhance a child's self-worth, seeing someone older who is open to learning is also an excellent lesson in and of itself: it's never too late to learn, and teachers aren't always the ones standing in front of the chalk board.

Caretaker. More and more grandparents are called upon to offer actual physical care for grandchildren. With the numbers of working parents and the lack of adequate day care so prevalent, many grandparents are becoming day-to-day caretakers for their grandchildren. This is often a necessity, and can have negative consequences in terms of requiring grandparents to take on a more parental role, thus missing out on some of the previously mentioned "unfettered" time together, but this can be mitigated to some extent (for more discussion of grandparents who become primary caretakers, see the section on Meeting Special Challenges). Even if your family is fortunate enough not to need you to perform this role, it can be great when grandparents can provide care for short periods of time, a few hours at a stretch, giving parents a much needed break and some time to go ahead and do something special for themselves.

Magician. Our grandchildren can't figure out how Grandpa does his magic tricks, or how Grandma always has cookies in the cookie jar and a nickel in her purse. One night, coming home, I was riding in the back seat with one of my grand-children who was cranky and tired. I made up a little trick to distract him and keep him busy for the rest of the car ride. It wasn't very sophisticated, to say the least. The next day, on a walk, he looked up at me and said, "Grandma, I think I figured out the magic trick." I asked him what the secret was. "I can't tell you because then it would be over," he said. "I'd rather remember you as doing magic."

It always felt to me that my grandmother was magic because she knew when I needed a hug or a smile, she always had change in her coin purse, and could make good food so easily, and she knew how to make people happy. In other words, what was most magic about my grandmother was the dependability of her giving personality. Dependability and familiarity, mixed in with just a little bit of wonder ("How did you know?" or "How did you do that?"), can often feel special. And having some tiny presents or surprises or "tricks" that are always there, whether in your cookie jar, glove compartment, pocket, purse, or even in how you interact with your grandchild, can give some sense that life can be magical.

Potentially Conflictual Aspects of the Influential Link

Virginia Satir, a pioneer in family systems therapy, once said that every situation presents an opportunity and a handicap. I mentioned earlier that grandparenting can also carry with it some potential for conflict.

Setting Negative Examples. As a professional psychologist, I have specialized in the area of addictions. Just as grandparents can be positive in the role models they provide grandchildren, they can also have a negative influence. For example, countless studies have shown that the addictions of nicotine, alcohol, food, and drugs, can be highly "familial." Leaving aside the issue of genetics in addiction, I am referring here to the obvious role-modeling that goes on within families. Therapists see families of drinkers, smokers, food addicts, and substance abusers. If any of these behaviors is affecting your family, it would be in everyone's best interest to seek outside professional help, and, hopefully, provide your grandchildren a better choice for their own futures. Needless to say, there are many other negative behaviors a grandparent can model, including violence, physical or sexual abuse, an inability to deal with emotions, an inability to respect boundaries, disrespect for other people and/or their property and privacy... The important thing to remember is that children look to adults and learn from what they see. Imagining the example you set for your grandchildren can be a new way to see yourself, and can provide a new opportunity to try to correct what you don't like or what doesn't seem to be working. Again, if the problem is serious enough, professional help is probably the best solution. Less dramatic behavior modification can be achieved on your own, starting with heightening your self-awareness.

Evoking Old Conflicts between Parents and Grandparents. Another handicap grandchildren sometimes have to suffer through is the excess emotional baggage that can exist between their parents and their grandparents. There are many situations and events that can result in unfinished business or stress in the relationship between adult children, who are often parents themselves, and their parents. If there is ongoing stress or tension between you and your children, or if there has been an actual break in the relationship, then the lesson being passed on to the grandchildren is that relationships, even within families, do not have lasting value, that it is okay for conflicts to go unresolved, and that abandonment and distancing are acceptable means of coping with conflict.

It is important for adults to find as much tolerance and compromise as they possibly can in order to allow grandchildren to thrive without being caught in the midst of conflicts they do not understand, suffering consequences they did nothing to produce.

Provoking New Conflicts between Parents and Grandparents. Whereas most of the time a vital, active grandparent is welcomed by children and grandchildren alike, there can be strains around the issue of grandparents maintaining their own lives. Some families believe grandparents should always be available (after all, they aren't tied down by children or jobs), and should even have available disposable income to share.

It is important for parents of young children to recognize that their own parents have already done their job of parenting, and have fulfilled their caretaking roles in this way. After years of working, the time and money these individuals spend on themselves is appropriate. What they choose to share with their children and grandchildren at this point is pure gift.

Still, parents can become resentful when they see their own parents spoiling grandchildren, perhaps providing them with extras they never got when they were growing up. In my own experience, as I mentioned earlier, I had less money and time to spend on my children when they were growing up than I do today. I am very lucky to have some financial security and some freedom with my time now. I can share these with my grandchildren, and I love to. On the other hand, although spoiling children, materially or otherwise, has long been considered a grandparent's prerogative, it's really important that grandparents not spoil to such a degree that the child's parents feel upstaged or defied. And remember, presence is more important than presents.

In terms of spending time or helping care for grandchildren, one grandmother I know went to an aerobics class every morning. Her daughter resented this tremendously, and was jealous of the "free" time her mother had to do something for herself when she could have been baby sitting her grandchildren, and thus freeing up the daughter's time. It's absolutely natural for such feelings to arise, just as it's natural for an older person to want to take care of herself and her own needs. It can help if adult children who are also parents remember that their own parents have earned their places in life. If

Presence is more important than presents.

they can offer their parents this respect, without behaving as though they are now entitled to all that a grandparent may provide them as well as their children, they may just be surprised at how much is offered out of pure generosity and desire. For their part, grandparents should remember that parenting is hard work, and that anything they can do to help their children out during this time has the potential to help everyone: by providing the grandchild with more contact or support, by decreasing the burden on the parent and thus making home life for both parent and child a happier experience, and by providing themselves with yet another opportunity to make an even deeper connection to grandchildren. Once again, compromise is key.

The ABCs of Trust:
Affection, Boundaries, and Confidences

Positive, healthy relationships, even within a family, don't just happen. One of the most important components of a good relationship — perhaps even the most important — is trust. Trust is never to be taken for granted; even with babies or young children, it has to be established. As the adult, it is a grandparent's responsibility to earn and maintain a child's trust by demonstrating respect.

One of the key arenas for establishing this trust and displaying respect is around physical boundaries. Now we all know that there's no feeling on earth that beats the spontaneous, unsolicited physical affection of a child. But there are also not many feelings worse than being physically overwhelmed or overpowered by someone who's bigger than you are.

In our eagerness to love our grandchildren, many grandparents overstep boundaries with affection, especially with younger children. With adult strength we tend to grab, hug, and kiss grandchildren without checking to see whether these actions are even welcome. *Show your grandchildren that you respect their physical privacy and autonomy by making sure they want to be physical with you before you become physical with them.*

Every child knows how close he or she wants to be to any adult, including a grandparent. And familiar or not, sometimes a grandparent's size, strength, scent, or style can be scary and overpowering to a child. It's really important to be sensitive to this possibility. Some healthy ways to handle demonstrating your affection include building an emotionally trusting relationship before even expecting for a physical demonstration of love or affection; offering a handshake or smile to a child who seems shy and working up to a hug; and *asking* the child for a kiss or hug, completely backing off if he or she shows any hesitation. Not every child is the same; some are more shy or more outgoing than others. And any child may go through moods of feeling differently at some times than at others. The thing to remember is that kids need to feel autonomous, especially about their bodies. They need to know that no one, not even a grandparent, has a *right* to touch them, and that they can be as affectionate or non-affectionate as they choose *without risking losing your love.*

Another area in which it's important to establish a trusting relationship is not physical, but personal. You may be lucky enough to develop relationships with your grandchildren that are close enough for them to confide in you, even if you're a long-distance grandparent.

When this is the case, it's tremendously important for you to respect the confidentiality of your relationship with your grandchild. Remember that grandparents can feel much safer to children than parents; because they don't fear your judgement or punishment, and because they know from experience that you won't be as critical, the kids may tell you things they wouldn't dream of telling their parents.

Even if the content of the confidence turns out to be something seemingly unimportant, and terrifically adorable to boot, you must never break the trust of that child by reporting back what was said to the parents. If the child were ever to discover that you betrayed his or her trust, it could be extremely difficult, if not impossible, to regain.

If a child of any age tells you something which you determine is so serious that the parents really must be informed, tell your thoughts about this to the child first. With your encouragement, he or she may be willing to go to his or her parents alone; if you still sense hesitation, you could offer to talk to the parents together with the child.

Always remember that the kind of trusting relationship you share is a gift, and that you want to keep the lines of communication open for as long as you are going to be in each other's lives.

Disciplining Grandchildren

Because I am alone so often with my grandchildren, and because they often visit me in my home, it's inevitable that there will be times when I'll have to discipline them. Grandchildren should never be caught between their parents and their grandparents, especially around matters of discipline. Because parents are primarily responsible for child-rearing, it is extremely important for grandparents to respect the rules and boundaries set by parents, and to see that children observe those rules and boundaries even when their parents aren't present. It's also important to learn how to discipline our grandchildren in a way that feels right for us.

All kids need to know they can't do certain things like running in front of cars, hurting their younger siblings (or any one else, for that matter), or behaving rudely.

If the children are in danger of hurting themselves or someone else, it's important to be firm with them. In less acute circumstances, such as wanting to stay up past bedtime, not wanting to participate in a planned activity, or rude behavior, it's just as important to negotiate compromises.

Different Rules for Different Houses. The rules in the children's home may be much more relaxed than the rules you want to see observed in your own home. On the other hand, you may find some of the rules set up by the children's parents to be more rigid than those you would set. Ultimately, there are two "rules of thumb" to follow: 1) unless they put the child in an unsafe situation, parents' rules for a child ought to be observed in or out of the parents' home, and 2) you should not be made uncomfortable in your own home.

For example, at this point in my life, I don't have young children running through my house everyday, so I keep lots of things sitting out in my house within easy reach of children, things which might break easily. Now, when my grandchildren come to my house, one of my jobs is to make the environment safe for them by making certain that anything which could be dangerous — objects that are sharp or easily swallowed, toxic cleaning supplies, medicines, tools, etc. — are safely out of reach. But a second job is to teach the children the difference between being at home, where they can play almost everywhere because it's a house set up for children, and the special rules that apply when they come to Grandma's house.

I'll never forget seeing my three year-old grandson headed to crawl on my living room table... At his house, the living room table is also a road to toy cars, a surface for drawing with crayons, and a general activity center for the children. At my house, the table holds fresh flowers in a vase and dainty ceramic butterflies. When Matthew headed to my table to begin crawling all over it, he got one knee up there, turned around, saw my face, and said, "Uh oh. I can only climb on tables at my house, right Grandma?"

"Right, Matthew," I said.

And he learned something.

In a kind of reverse example, it also became important for me to let the kids know I respected the rules established by their parents. In the early days of grandparenting, I wanted to become known as the *"M & M"* Grandma — I kept a jar of the candies in my cupboard. Needless to say the kids loved this, and I felt okay about it because I felt that the children needed treats.

It didn't take very long before my daughter shared with me her belief that children should have a limited amount of sugar because too much is unhealthy for them. The next time her son came to visit and wanted his usual fistful of *M & Ms,* I had to tell him he could have two at the beginning of his visit, and two before he went home, but that was all the *M & Ms* he was getting because that was what his Mom said.

He looked at me. "But Grandma says I can have more."

Now right then and there I had to make a decision. Did his relationship with his mother take precedence over his desire to have Grandma give him something?

"You can have the amount of *M & Ms* and other treats that Mom says you can have. We have to do what Mom thinks is best."

He learned to accept this very quickly, and without very much heartache at all.

As much emphasis as I've placed on offering grandchildren unconditional love and support, it's also important for a grandparent *not* to become the person who gives all the treats and kisses all the sores. Not only can this potentially rob the child's parents of some of the opportunities for providing love and comfort, but it can also unfairly put parents who do have to discipline children in the position of being "the bad guys."

One other important thing to remember is that although conventional wisdom says that spoiling grandchildren is one of the wonderful privileges of being a grandparent (vs. being a parent, whose job it often is to teach their children that they can't have everything they want), the relatively occasional times when you will have to discipline a grandchild or say "No" can actually make your relationship with the child healthier. Grandparents who do more than just indulge their grandchildren may have to endure a few moments of the child's discontent here and there, but as they get older, you may find you've set the foundation for a fuller, less one-dimensional relationship, and by setting boundaries, which are healthy and important for children, you will be doing something positive.

Dealing with Anger: The Time-Out or Think-About-It Chair. One of my greatest ongoing questions about my own grandparenting skills involves how well I communicate with my grandchildren when they cause me to become angry or distressed.

I've actually learned a great deal about disciplining children from my own daughters now that they're parents themselves. In our family, it's become traditional to talk about "the time-out chair" or "the think-about-it-chair." Any chair in the house can become the think-about-it chair when you need it to.

My current approach for handling a situation that has made me angry or upset is to simply distance myself, and to cease any activity that had been going on. I explain to the child that I am uncomfortable or angry, and that I need to stop the activity or inter-action right now.

Remember, anger is a valid, healthy signal that something which is going on doesn't feel good. It's important to let children know that it's okay if they get angry, and it's okay if you get angry, as long as no one acts out the angry feelings with physical violence against another. It's also important to note that saying "I'm very angry" is a really different statement, and sends a very different mes-sage, than "You made me angry." Also, children need to know that anger is okay, and that you will get over your anger. So this is a time when the chairs can be a help.

"I'm very angry right now. I need to stop when I'm angry, and perhaps you do too, so I think we should both go to our think-about-it chairs and sit by ourselves quietly for a few minutes." If this seems too extreme for the situation at hand, or if you are out in public where there are no chairs available to use for this purpose, or if the child seems unwilling or unable to sit still and be quiet, then the least you should do is be sure to stop whatever activity you were engaged in together when you or the child got mad.

Traditions and Rituals

Some believe families that celebrate traditions and rituals together are happier than those that do not. In today's society, with so many families scattered geographically and so many family members having multiple obligations and pressures on their time, this can be especially important. A family's identity, as well as its strength and self-worth, can be nourished by the deep sense of connectedness and history that traditions and rituals can bring. Having family members come together in meaningful ways over time can strengthen family bonds and enrich individual family members' sense of rootedness and personal history.

Rituals may range from pleasurable activities (an annual "Ice Cream Sundaes for Sunday Dinner") to more spiritual observations (a Sabbath meal; a celebration of freedom on Martin Luther King, Jr., Day or at Passover). They may combine pleasure and something deeper. A family hike or camping trip — during which everyone gets to enjoy the beauty, health benefits, and connectedness to nature that comes from the activity itself — can also include a more directed sharing experience. At a designated time everyone can gather to share around a theme such as an ongoing problem in the family, an ongoing tragedy in the world, feelings or memories around a common loss of a loved family member or friend, or the joy around a new addition to the family.

The fact is that all families have unique traditions based on ethnic heritage, religion, and/or individual personalities. The kind of rituals a family observes is not as important as the fact that they are a regular part of life together as a family. Again, rituals help a family create memories and a sense of continuity and joy, a sense of being special. All of these contribute to individual self-worth as well as to the family's. As a grandparent, you can take the initiative to make sure that some of these rituals are established and continued.

Below are some suggestions for initiating and maintaining your family's specific rituals, those which aren't typically linked to religious observances.

1. *Give each tradition a name.* Whether you identify Happy Non-Birthday, Black Hills Summer Camp, the Las Vegas Extravaganza, Ice Cream Dinner, giving family traditions a name can formalize the tradition itself and help establish the event as something significant rather than accidental circumstance.

2. *Listen to all members of the family, including children, to offer ideas or indicate the potential for turning any occasion into a tradition.* "We always do it this way," or "Let's do this every year," or "Mom loves it when we bring her breakfast in bed

on her birthday," may be casual remarks about things that have happened only on occasion. But maybe occasions which have brought people pleasure can be turned into regular events so that people know they can count on this happiness with some regularity.

3. *Make a commitment to take traditions seriously.* Many people have said that if there is one predictor of good mental health, it's a feeling of being connected. Whether traditions take the form of a big family picnic every summer or children always receiving ice cream cones following piano lessons or birthdays always involving breakfast in bed or everybody taking a big camping trip together or the observation of religious holidays or phone calls to parents on Saturday mornings or making gifts instead of buying them or everybody contributing a different dish at Thanksgiving Dinner or particular foods that are always featured at certain occasions, it's important that people observe the traditions in a committed regular fashion, but also that everyone involved have enough flexibility that the traditions themselves don't become rigid, forced obligations.

Remember, traditions and rituals reveal a family's values, style, and heritage, and they reflect family members' commitment to each other. And the range of a family's rituals reflects the range of their ways of being with each other: playful, serious, instructive, spiritual, recreational, physically active... the more variety, the richer the whole tradition of *family* you pass along.

Some Special Notes on
Family Reunions as a Tradition

Often families will get together at least once a year. Some do this at special holidays such as Thanksgiving or Christmas; others choose yet another time of year so as not to interfere with individual family obligations that come through marriages and in-laws, work, or friends. It can also be more expensive to travel around the holidays, and if you have relatives coming together from far afield locales, this can be a factor.

The most important thing is to have as many family members as possible be part of a family reunion. It's also important that one person not assume all of the responsibility for putting the event together. Assign and delegate certain tasks. In my family, we've had reunions where one person was in charge of games, another was in charge of food, and still another was in charge of music. Everyone's particular gifts and skills can become part of the time you share together.

At a reunion we had for people of many different ages, we had a small swimming pool in the backyard for the little kids where they could splash around and have fun. I have even been extravagant enough on occasion to hire a masseuse for some of the older people at a reunion. If we've all taken a hike or gone horseback riding or bike riding, a massage can be a wonderful and relaxing luxury. And in my family, it seems as though we always have one or two people at a reunion who are pregnant, and so can't participate in the more vigorous activities. For them we might have some kind of card or board game tournament going on. Have a variety available. Every family has some special cooks — I've asked people to bring their best recipes or come prepared to do some cooking at the reunion.

Not only to make certain everyone feels incuded, but also because there are different activites more appropriate to different times of day, it's important that there be a range of activities available. Games that can be played by larger groups, such as Trivial Pursuit, can be fun in the evenings when things are quieting down. We might have some sing-alongs, or performances by family musicians or even friends whom you might want to invite to join you so that you can benefit from their talents and their company.

One of the best things about traditions are the memories they yield. But it can also be really nice to have a record — photographs or video recordings of time your family has gotten together. Photographs and recollections from family gatherings can also become part of your special Family History Project. "Assigning" people to be in charge of taking pictures or shooting video can be one more way to make sure everyone is involved or contributing.

What It Means to Be "Grand"

A friend once told me that her own grandmother existed for her as a role model of what *not* to be. She showed absolutely no interest in her grandchildren, and even resented the idea that she had them. To her they were a sign of her own aging, and just one more responsibility and bother. Her daughter, who had already suffered rejection and abandonment from her mother, looked to an aunt to be a substitute grandmother for her children — she thought of this woman as a "Grandaunt."

Though I was blessed in my life to have my Grandma Olson, I was also blessed with aunts who had learned nurturing skills and who could, I think, qualify as "Grandaunts." They shared their ideas and wisdom with me, and guided me through many stages of my life. As I grew older, often making unpopular decisions and choices, these women continued to love me and to accept who I was becoming. Most importantly, I remember their houses and the sense of welcome and belonging that I felt there. I now realize I've tried to duplicate that spirit in my home, and offer not only to my children and grandchildren, but to all who come to visit, a sense of belonging, a sense that for them, there is always room to spare and food to eat. Providing this nurturing and comfort is one aspect of grandparenting, but it's a skill anyone can learn, and it needn't be reserved for grandchildren. It's a loving way of being. I have seen both men and women, with and without biological grandchildren, come to learn and practice these skills.

It must also be acknowledged that there are countless foster grandparents and self-appointed grandparents, grandaunts, granduncles, brothers, sisters, and friends who bring this dimension into the lives of children. (In turn, children can bring joy to elders. Adopt-a-Grandparent is a program established in Florida in 1963 which involves weekly class visits by young children to nursing homes. Variations of this kind of program sprang up all around the country.) Whatever your role in the child's life, remember that you can be "grand."

> Whatever your role in the child's life, remember that you can be "grand."

A Note on In-Laws

I'm including in this section just a few words on relating to your children in-law, though certainly the ideas here apply to your relationships with them even when you're not visiting with each other in person.

It's very important to pay attention to your sons- and daughters-in-law. All of us have special relationships with our own children which, hopefully, have become even closer as we and they have gotten older. It can be difficult, however, for us to find a special place with our sons- and daughters-in-law, or for them to feel close to us. Sometimes it's the eldest person's job to initiate the development of a better relationship.

I remember when my daughters first got married and I would call them, the same thing would happen in both houses. If the husband answered the phone, he'd say "Oh hi, Sharon, I bet you're calling for Debby (or Sandy)," and then hand the phone to my daughter. This was a habit we all fell into pretty easily, but I wasn't happy about it — I wanted to feel closer to the men my daughters had married. But it was only when my grandchildren were born that this actually began to happen. Once there were grandchildren, I was calling not just to speak to my daughters, but to find out how the babies were. I began talking to the children's fathers about what was new as easily as I would my daughters. Eventually this led to having more conversations with these men about themselves, and about myself.

In the past few years, I've noticed that it really doesn't matter who answers the phone when I call, because even if I get to speak with my daughters first, I'll also want to talk to my sons-in-law.

This can be even more important as grandchildren begin to get a little older — you don't want to have a three-generational relationship that excludes one of the children's parents! Some ways to get to know your children-in-law once grandchildren have arrived include asking them what they enjoy most about parenting, what scares them, and even how things are going at work. Try to find out about their lives in general — who are their friends? What do they enjoy? It's also alright to ask them how they feel about the relationship that you all share as family, and whether there's anything else that you can do to make things go more smoothly, or to feel closer.

The better friend you are to your in-law children, the better it is for the whole family.

Meeting
Special
Challenges

When one door of happiness closes, another opens. Often we look so long at the closed door that we do not see the one which has been opened for us.

— HELEN KELLER

In loving healthy families, parents and grandparents are there to meet the needs of the child. In hurting, painful families, children get used to meeting the needs of their parents and grandparents. This is true even, and perhaps especially, when families face difficulties. Several challenges that families may face are addressed in this section, which isn't meant to be exhaustive because these certainly aren't the only troubles a family may encounter. Still, the ideas presented here may be appropriate for other situations as well. Perhaps the most important message in this section is that children should never feel as though they are the grown-ups in the family, or as though they have to assume adult responsibilities. Crises and painful situations are hard on everyone, but children need to feel as safe as possible just the same. They need to be taken care of by adults. And grandparents can always help.

When a Grandparent Isn't Well

For some children, a grandparent's illness is the first time they have to deal with a major loss. When a grandparent loses the ability to do certain things (travel, go to the beach, drive a car, cook meals, etc.), it may even be frightening to a child. It's best to be honest with children, though there's no need to expose them to unnecessary details. But a grandparent can acknowledge what's going on, and how things are different now from the way they used to be. This can help children feel less frightened by the changes. Also, if the grandparent can model some comfort level with his or her illness, this will help children feel more comfortable, both by allowing them to continue to feel close to the grandparent, and by making illness itself less foreign and foreboding. Again, grandparents can speak openly with their grandchildren about no longer being able to do certain things that used to be possible, and talk about whether the changes are temporary or permanent. Children should be encouraged to ask questions and express feelings, and grandparents should provide as much reassurance as is possible without avoiding the truth.

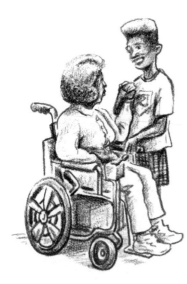

If a grandparent's mobility and/or activity level is seriously restricted by an illness or injury, he or she can continue to communicate and connect with grandchildren in as many ways as possible, including phone calls and letters and messages, often via parents, and continue to let grandchildren know that they are still in their thoughts.

Death

As with illness, sometimes a grandparent's death is the first loss of someone close that a child experiences. But not always. Whatever the circumstances, grandparents who are alive and able must be prepared to "be there" for grandchildren when a death occurs, to talk, to comfort, and to be honest. If you were close to the person who has died, then you will be dealing with your own grief, too. Try not to let this get in the way of being emotionally available to your grandchildren as they navigate this painful loss. You may even discover that helping them manage the death of someone close to you both can help you, too.

And again, as with illnesses, it's important that children feel free to ask questions and learn to talk about feelings. Let children know that it's absolutely okay to experience and express a whole range of feelings when someone dies, including fear, sadness, hurt, and anger. Tears should be welcomed rather than discouraged at times of sorrow.

It's equally important that children understand that death is a natural part of life, and so not to be feared. Each family's ways of explaining death reflect their own belief system and traditions. Whatever your family's practices, don't leave the child or children out of conversations. This promotes isolation and loneliness. Some other suggestions include the following:

✓ **Don't** always associate death with disease or old age. This can make children afraid when they are ill, and promote fear of aging.

✓ **Don't** say death is like sleep. In addition to confusing children about the possibility of someone who is dead "waking up," this can also promote fear of sleep.

✓ **Do,** as mentioned, encourage children to talk about their feelings.

✓ **Do** find ways to help children keep their memories of whomever has died alive. Memories are a healing, loving link between those who have died and those who still live.

✓ **Do,** whenever possible, begin teaching children about death before they have to confront it. Many children will develop an interest, even a fascination, with death around the age of three or four, even if they have not known personally someone who has died. They may ask all sorts of questions, some of which are even funny to grown-ups because they seem to not quite grasp the concept of death. It's important to be as honest and as clear in responding to these questions as possible.

There are books available that can be helpful.

• *How Do We Tell the Children: Helping Children Understand and Cope When Someone Dies* (Authors: Dan Schaefer & Christine Lyons. Publisher: Newmarket Press). An outstanding book for adults that will tell you what children aged two and older already know and are capable of understanding about death. It can help guide you in what to say and how to say it in order to help children deal with grief.

- *The Cat Next Door.* (Author: Betty Ren Wright. Publisher: Holiday House Publisher). Grandma dies but her grandchild remembers her in a "splendiferous" way. A warm and appealing story that tells of the closeness between grandchild and grandparent. Recommended for pre-school aged children.

- *Alex the Kid with AIDS.* (Author: Linda Walvoord Girard. Publisher: Albert Whitman & Co.). Alex has contracted AIDS from a blood transfusion. His fourth grade classmates learn he can be a good friend and a regular guy. With a compassionate and humorous touch, the book shows how a very real child reacts to having a terrible disease, and how others react to him. Recommended for ages 7-10 years.

There are many wonderful books for children and adolescents that address a wide range of sensitive topics. Ask your local bookseller or librarian.

The following letters were written by three teenagers to their grandfather when they knew he was dying. Clearly these children were informed, and very capable of handling the truth about their grandfather's impending death. This allowed them to say goodbye, an opportunity not everyone gets, and to express their feelings to "Poppy" directly. (It's interesting how much he was loved for having been a teacher to these children.)

Poppy,

I am very sorry that we could not come down to see you this time, but I know I will see you again soon. I pray that god is taking care of you and keeping you out of pain. I want you to know that you have been a great influence in my life, and always will be. You gave so much of your love and guidance to us, and I want you to know how much I love you for that. All of the wisdom you shared with me has found a permanent place in my heart. We have a special and beautiful relationship that many people have never had the joy of experiencing. You are the best grandfather in the world and I want you to know that all of the wonderful memories you have given me, and all the knowledge you have passed on to me, will live with me forever. I love you deeply, Poppy. Your the best.

Always,

Melissa

© MORGAN, INC.

Poppy,

Hey, how are you doing? I just want to let you know how sorry I am that I can't visit you with my Mom. If there was any way I could, believe me, I would. Throughout the years you have shown me many things and I have learned a great deal from you. All the advice you've given us kids was wonderful. I love you to an extent that can't be written in words. Just always know that you are the best Grandad a girl could ask for. I just finished taking my 6-weeks test, and I know I did well. I hope everything's going alright on your end. How Nana? Everything here is okay except the fact that I don't get to see you as much as I'd like to. Well, I'd better let you go.

I love you with all my heart,
Marina

P.S. Always know, Poppy, that all your efforts at being a Grandad are acknowledged by me and I thank you.

Dear Poppy,

Yesterday I heard the news of your health from my sister. She also told me about how we were going to go see you. I was happy that I was going to see you, but I was also worried that might not be the best thing for either of us. I don't think I could bear to see you in so much pain. I also know that it would be stressful on you if my sisters and I were to go. I would like to let you know that I am doing much better in school and will always remember the wonderful things that you taught me through the years. I cherish the moments we spent together, and will always think of you as the absolute best grandpa a kid could ever have. It always comforts me to think that you are going to a much better place and will be totally be free of pain.

I now know that I will not be able to see you again and believe that it may be better for both of us. To sum it all up I would like to say that I love you with all the love in the world. I will always be thinking of you and how happy you will be with the Lord. You don't have to worry, I'll take care of Nanna for you. Not one day will pass that I won't anticipate being with you and Uncle Al once again in heaven. Your time has come and now it is time for me to let you go. My Mom will give you all my love.

    With all the love my heart could hold,
    Michael

P.S. Thank you for the many wonderful things you gave me. I shall cherish them always along with the many special memories of the time we spent together. Good Bye.

Divorce

It would seem as though divorce occurs between two adults, but if there are children involved, divorce really happens to the whole family. How does everyone cope?

Usually all family behaviors are exaggerated at times of high stress. Those who have good coping skills will continue to use them. Examples include asking for support from family and friends, getting help from a professional therapist, taking care of oneself (maintaining good nutrition, getting enough exercise and sleep), protecting some "alone time" and peaceful solitude, and treating oneself periodically (to a movie, dinner out, a day off, etc.).

Those with poor coping skills such as smoking, excessive eating, drinking, or other use of substance to 'medicate' one's pain or lethargy, may need to seek help from an outside therapist before the secondary reaction to the divorce situation becomes itself a primary problem.

In addition to the issues for the people in the primary family, there is also the pain involved in relationships with extended family members. Children of divorce also often feel pulled between their parents, and end up without a safe, trusted, secure place in either home, with either parent. It just may be that the strongest center is with a grandparent. Yet in my own work as a family therapist, I have observed again and again the heartbreak that children of divorce experience around being newly separated from a formerly close grandparent.

When both parents share concern for the children and allow and support the grandparents' involvement, the security and comfort the grandchildren receive is without measure. Too often, however, feelings of competition, jealousy, hurt, and anger rear up, and the grandparents become embroiled in these dynamics. When this is the case, the grandchildren are the major losers. As a therapist and as a grandparent, I always urge all adults involved in a divorce to be aware of the needs of the children and young people involved.

Grandparents can provide a sense of constancy for the child during this time of change, and reassure children that although painful things seem to be going on with Mom and Dad, everything is going to remain the same between grandparent and grandchild.

It's extremely important that grandparents not take sides during a divorce. The temptation can be great — one of the people involved is your own child. But the first and foremost task is to preserve your relationship with your grandchild or grandchildren, and to do everything you can to ensure that this relationship can continue.

It may be a good idea at the time of a separation or divorce for everyone to sit down in one room and talk about what is best for whom. Regardless of whether children are old enough to participate in this kind of discussion or "negotiation," loving parents and grandparents will talk this through. It should be agreed among everyone that the divorce is not the business of the children or of the grandparents, but you can certainly let everyone know how important it is that the grandparent-grandchildren relationships continue. And though it may involve more time, money, or energy to continue the relationships between grandparents and grandchildren during a separation or following a divorce, its importance cannot be emphasized

> *During a divorce... the first and foremost task is to preserve your relationship with your grandchild or grandchildren.*

enough; it may be one of the best investments a family can make. Do whatever seems necessary, including seeking professional help, in order to work through this difficult situation.

Some practical suggestions for grandparents:

✓ **Don't** take sides.

✓ **Don't** use the children for emotional support. Get outside, professional help for yourself.

✓ **Don't** postpone closeness in a relationship for later when everything is settled and worked out.

✓ **Don't** live only in the pain of the moment.

✓ **Don't** dwell on the past or on the way it used to be. Let these times be released.

✓ **Don't** live in resentment. It hurts everyone involved, especially you.

✓ **Do** refrain from judging either parent.

✓ **Do** offer emotional support and listen carefully to feelings.

✓ **Do** find the time and money to invest in a close relationship now, when the children need it.

✓ **Do** try to share some fun times with the children.

✓ **Do** try to build some future goals, a trip, a special new kind of holiday, a way to stay connected, etc.

✓ **Do** find whatever ways you need in order to forgive.

If it's not possible to work with your children and grandchildren, you are going to need a great deal of support, and maybe even some legal education, about your feelings, your choices, and your rights. Begin by seeking help from a competent family therapist and/or legal aid.

If the divorce is leaving the children completely without contact with one of their parents, they are also going to be missing a role model of that gender. If a father leaves his children, those kids may need a transitional or even more permanent male role model. If a mother leaves, the same is true for a female role model. Grandparents may "fill in" in this respect, and so make an important contribution.

Sometimes grandparents can also help financially. Things are usually a lot tougher economically for a family following a divorce. If possible, maybe you can help with expenses — braces, insurance, even special, positive gifts such as bikes. If you are fortunate enough to be able to help in this way, it's important to work closely with the parent(s) in order to do so in a way that is consensual. It is not in the best interest of anyone for grandparents to take over or become Santa Claus or saviors. It isn't fair to the parents, and it isn't healthy for the children. Always remember that these are your grandchildren and not your children, even when they're hurting, and even when circumstances are depriving them or causing them pain.

In the context of a divorce or at any other time, if you ever believe that something is happening which is harmful to your grandchild or grandchildren, such as parents' drug use, abandonment or neglect, or physical or sexual abuse, you will need both

therapeutic help and legal counseling. For the sake of your grand-children, don't hold back. This is an appropriate time to intervene.

Grandma Ann & Grandpa Bill

Our relationship with our granddaughter Katie began long before she was born. Our son and his wife were ending their marriage when they discovered she was pregnant. They made the courageous decision to commit to being good parents to this little life-to-be, even if they were parting ways.

Of course we were worried by questions and concerns about how such an unconventional arrangement might work. As ex-in-laws, would we get to see our first grandchild? Would she be damaged by not having married parents?

We also felt extremely proud of our son for his mature commitment to fatherhood. The moment he called to tell us that the baby had been born, we loved her. When we finally got to see her she was a beautiful Christmas present. We were in love! There, in our ex-daughter-in-law's home with her parents and our son, we were all united by our love of little Kathryn Ann.

She is five years old now. She has many relatives and spends time traveling from Mom's house to Dad's house and among her grandparents. There is a great deal of love for this child to receive, and having her to love has been a great lesson for us. We have learned to be flexible and tolerant. We have learned that families are unique, and that many kinds of families can work successfully.

"And a little child shall lead them...."

Grandparents Who Become Their Grandchildren's Parents

Some grandparents must, out of necessity, become parents or parent figures when grandchildren's parents are unable or unwilling to care for them. According to the U.S. Census, in 1992, almost 3.3 million children lived in a home maintained by a grandparent. Of those, 867,000, or about 1.3% of the nation's youth, lived with grandparents without a parent present at all.

Whatever circumstances may necessitate such an arrangement, grandparents who find themselves functioning as parents face many stresses. For their own sakes, and for the sakes of their grandchildren, they need as much support as possible.

A network of support groups known as *ROCKING* (Raising Our Children's Kids) can help. They can be reached at (616) 683-2058.

Also, *AARP* (American Association of Retired Persons) has opened a Grandparent Information Center to help second-time-around parents cope with legal, financial, and emotional problems. They offer tips on concerns ranging from locating baby sitting help to legally adopting a grandchild. Contact your local chapter, or reach them at their national offices at (202) 434-2296.

Grandparents Raising Grandchildren is a non-profit organization that offers emotional support and political muscle to grandparents who are primary caregivers. Write P.O. Box 104, Colleyville, TX

76034 for information about the organizations, legal issues, and support groups in your community.

Finally, *Grandparents As Parents* will help grandparents find or start a support group in their area. Write to 1150 East 4th Street, Suite #221, Long Beach, CA 90802.

Adopted or Step-Grandchildren

In today's world, there are many kinds of families, including, among others, those with single parents, those with two working parents, combined families, and families with adopted children.

The important thing to remember with adopted or step-grandchildren is that they are tremendously wanted and cherished by your own child. Chances are that with enough love, the biological ties won't make that much difference to the children; they shouldn't make any difference to the grandparents either.

If you let nature and instinct take over, it will. Who can resist eyes that look into yours with trust, or a smile that breaks wide open when you speak, or a little hand that reaches for your own? Once you dry a child's tears or nurse them through an illness, share a secret or laughter, or experience the many gentle, genuine ways the child can express care for *you*, you will feel bonded. Let it happen. These are the kinds of ties that humanize us all.

When there are siblings involved, there can be extra stress, conflictual feelings, and painful confusion about how to feel. Remember, you can be a helpful role model at such times. By welcoming the new child into your family, and by reassuring your biological grandchildren that you still love them just as much as you did before and that nothing and no one can ever change how uniquely special they are to you, you will be sending all the right messages. Whatever their ages, spend time with all the kids together, and spend some individual time with each of them. Remember, you can have a relationship with each one of these young people, and you can be special to all of them.

When a Grandchild Has Special Needs

It has often been said that one never receives more than one can handle. Many grandparents have received the frightening news that a grandchild is suffering from a debilitating or fatal illness, or perhaps a handicap of some kind. Children can also develop mild to severe psychological conditions. The spectrum of special needs a child may have can range from a mild learning disability to a chronic illness, from a difference such as blindness or deafness to a fatal disease. Some conditions are congenital, others arise later. Some can arise for a time and resolve with good medical or psychological care. Regardless of the particulars, the first feelings that will come up for grandparents are usually sadness, hurt, anger, and fear. There are feelings for the grandchild, for the child's parent(s), and for oneself.

For families facing this level of severe crisis or chronic difficulty, the effects can be devastating. Some families can surmount these obstacles, however, and grandparents can play a significant and determining role in how families weather such adverse circumstances.

Grandparents can step in and offer additional support, whether financial, emotional, or physical. They can baby sit, arrange special times for a grandchild who is ill, or offer well children in the family — who may not be getting as much attention from everyone as does the less healthy or able child — some needed focus and time.

Networks and support groups for families with a child who has special needs exist nationally and locally. Social workers, teachers, counselors, therapists, and other professionals in your area should be able to put you and your family in contact with appropriate organizations.

* * *

It has been a blessing my life to have come into personal and professional contact with many, many people who have been willing to share their humanity and their human stories.

And although many of my friends have been fortunate enough to have grandchildren who are well, healthy and robust, many other friends have had to struggle with very special grandchildren, and with their very special needs. These people have had more difficult mountains to climb. In the next few pages, some of them share their struggles and their victories.

Three Stories of Grandmas
Helping Out Early On...

"There is something wrong with this baby, Mum. He is most unpleasant and miserable, not at all like the others." My lights went on — was my daughter actually comparing her baby to his siblings? After all the work I had done on my own childhood issues, I thought I had clearly taught my children not to compare. Strange that my reactions did not concern the baby, but my own real or imagined inadequacy as a parent. How egocentric can one get?

I am a grandparent of five grandchildren. The child about whom my daughter complained turned out to have a devastating disease — Tuberous Sclerosis. It is cruel how little is known about it. Tiny babies have seizures, and physicians have little information. "It's colic," said one pediatrician. I had thought so too until I witnessed a seizure, at which point I leapt to the phone and told this doctor in no uncertain terms that this was not colic. "There's nothing wrong with that baby," she said. "I examined him and he is neurologically sound." At the time of the next seizure, which took place in a health food store where I was certain a good diet would provide a cure, I knew the doctor was wrong. My daughter called her again, however, and again got the same response. So I called again. "Oh, no," said the doctor. "Don't tell me she has you fussing again now." When the final diagnosis came through, this doctor was mortified. In my book, there's no excuse for such callous behavior. I joined the National Tuberous Sclerosis Association and attended the international conference on genetic research. Bittersweet indeed. There is hope for the future with investi-

gations, but for us, uncertainty because of the early seizure activity. Being in recovery, I know how to take things one day at a time, and how to adjust to things over which I have no control. The brothers and sisters of this child are superb, and wonderful with him, but we have already seen the autistic components in his behavior, so I know that their lives are stressful daily.

I tell all of them that they are angels, gifts from the universe. Sometimes I think they think I have forgotten their names! I whisper in their ears that they are miracles, and that two of my supreme honors on this planet have been to be the mother of one of their parents, and to be their grandmother....

— Grandma Yvonne

After many hours of labor, my daughter Kim gave birth, five weeks early, to her first child, Paul. During her pregnancy, Kim had developed gestational diabetes, preclamptia/hypertension, and also an incompetent cervix, so we had not been without concern. During a routine ultrasound prior to Paul's birth, fluid was discovered in his intestine. Within 24 hours after the birth, he was taken to Children's Hospital for surgery to remove a bowel obstruction. During these trying hours, the families of both parents stood a prayerful watch for a successful outcome.

Every day of the four-month hospital stay which followed his surgery was a victory for tiny Paul. Four days following the first surgery, he underwent a second procedure to close a valve to the lungs which had compromised his breathing and the supply of oxygen to his brain. This second procedure took much more time than the first, and increased our prayers for God's intercession in Paul's struggles to survive. I often recall the hours Paul's family spent praying in the chapel together, with parents and grandparents of different faiths all confident our prayers would be heard.

Paul's four-month battle for life was strengthened by a mother, father, and grandparents whose devotion to him bonded us to each other. And a miracle unfolded before our eyes.

Paul is now six years old and in the first grade. This past December, as we approached the season of miracles, the family watched our own little miracle sing, dance, and recite his lines at his school Christmas play.

Paul has been an inspiration to many of those who have watched his life and his health evolve. He is living proof of God's love when faced with pain or crises. After all, our little miracle had no idea, when he was struggling to survive, how beautiful life could be.

— Grandma Elaine

I answered the phone to my son's sobs. "Mother, I need you. The baby isn't breathing or moving and they're going to do an emergency C-section. Please hurry — I need you!" Nothing could have stopped me. I arrived at the hospital to see my son terrified, in shock. I went to hold him and he pointed to the nursery and said, "Go to the baby; they'll let you in."

My grandson was in an incubator, hooked up to life-support machines. Tubes and IVs were taped to his little body, patches taped over his eyes. He weighed four pounds. As I looked at him, I became very aware that he needed to know that he was loved and wanted. It was apparent that he was fighting for his life. I wanted to be as close *as possible to him because I needed to talk to him. I pressed my hands and face to the plastic bubble and began to tell him how much he was loved, and how important he was to his new family. I told him I knew he was fighting to come into the family and that I was going to give him all the energy and strength I could in order to help. I had just said how much I would love to hold him so he could feel the love and strength I was sending him, when a miracle happened. The nurse came over and said I could hold him. "It can help when they're fighting for their lives." I was given boots, a cap, a gown, gloves, and a face mask to welcome my grandson into this world. What a sensation I experienced when I picked him up! I knew I was to help him gain strength. I sat in a rocking chair and began to rock and tell my grandson that he was entering a family of fighters. His Daddy, Grandpa, Grandma, aunts, and uncles had fought their way from the depths of addiction and depression and we had been waiting for him to join us and be able to love and be loved. I remembered hearing that singing soothes the soul, so I began singing my words to him. I could feel his little body responding and I knew that this tiny, precious, joy of my life was going to make it, and then I began to cry with gratitude. I have no idea how long I rocked and sang to him, but it felt as if it was just the two of us, working together, so he could join our family. Today he is the joy of my life.*

— Grandma Mary Lee

On the surface, it would seem as though the pain of trauma will wreak havoc on a family. All family members, including grandparents, may want to join an appropriate support group. Such groups diminish a sense of isolation by providing a place to share experiences with others who know just what you're going through, and who may be able to shed light on helpful approaches or simply listen to you with genuine sympathy; they can be also be helpful clearing houses of information about resources and current medical research. No one will deny the stress and trauma that can come with such difficulties, yet there are also opportunities. Children, parents, and grandparents can even form extra bonds with one another as they join to confront and cope with problems of health and development.

Grandparents should become familiar with any disabled child's difficulties. Learn how to talk about the subject knowledgeably. Read as much information as you can, and subscribe to publications that offer support and helpful suggestions. If a child is wheelchair-bound, be sure you know how to operate the chair, and how to move the child in and out of it. If a child requires certain clinical procedures at home on a regular basis (e.g., injections, other medications), you may want to be fully educated in how to administer these, the correct dosages, and any potential side effects. If the condition is psychological, you might offer to participate in some of the family therapy that may be going on. (Don't push this, however, and don't take it personally if your offer is declined — it may or may not be in the best interest of the child. If there is any conflict among family members about who should be present at family therapy sessions, let the therapist advise you.)

In addition to being able to help with the more trying aspects of the child's life, don't forget to focus also on this child's special qualities, and help build confidence and self-worth.

At the same time, be sure not to ignore the other children in the family who might be present. As mentioned earlier in this section, the demands of the special child might pull greatly and deprive healthier children in the family of attention they need. There is also the added dimension of guilt — healthy siblings of unwell children often experience guilt around being the "lucky" one, as well as anger because the ill or disabled sibling may get more attention. In the context of having a sick or disabled child, parents sometimes feel guilty about their hopes and dreams for their healthy children, and may pull away for this reason also. Siblings of children with special needs also have needs for their own focused, private times with parents and grandparents; these siblings must be assured that their needs are just as important, even if less urgent, than the needs of the child who isn't well, and that they are just as loved as ever.

Grandparents can help not only by spending caring time with these siblings, but by offering to care for the child with special needs so that the parents and the healthy children also can spend some quality time together.

Young People and Emotions

Overwhelming numbers of teens in this country today are wrestling with issues and decisions that affect their lives in significant ways: poverty, academic failure or dropping out, violence, substance abuse

and addiction, teen pregnancy, suicide, running away from home... If trends continue, the statistics will only get worse.

So, clearly, stress and anxiety are not restricted to adults. They can be, and usually are at one time or another, experienced by very young children, and by children who are older. Now, just by their natures, some kids will be more anxious than others. Some will act out their feelings in a variety of ways, including being very loud, bossy, disruptive, or disobedient. These kids can be extremely argumentative or competitive or aggressive. Some will act out their feelings in quieter ways, becoming moody or shy or fearful. These kids can end up being very fearful, or having developmental delays or signs of anxiety such as wetting the bed. Sources of stress and anxiety can vary greatly among children, even between siblings. For some, school may be the biggest problem. Others will have more difficulties with their social lives, including interactions with peers. Still others may feel tensions with parents from time to time, or more frequently. Some children experience real traumas, ranging from natural disasters to physical or sexual abuse to early loss to frightening accidents. Some children have to deal with the effects of poverty or racial tension in our society. For all children as they reach adolescence, identity issues — which can encompass the development of personal values and moral thinking, negotiating the physical milestones of puberty as well as their associated emotional and psychological effects, and developing a racial and sexual identity — become a challenge for young people. Whatever the source of the stress or the age of the child, expressing the feelings that result is an important part of good emotional health.

Thus, all children from all kinds of backgrounds, including very privileged ones, can use help gaining and developing skills for handling stress and anxiety. Perhaps the more our culture works to help young people at earlier ages — to nurture them, to listen to them, and to provide them with healthy models for behavior and relationships — the more we can prevent some of the potentially lethal problems that can occur as they get older and start to take more risks.

If our grandchildren can learn to *feel* what they are feeling, *express* how they are feeling, and *cope* with their feelings, later difficulties can be prevented or diminished. We as grandparents cannot eliminate destructive influences or ease all paths, but we can help young people develop skills necessary to better handle their feelings.

Communicating about Emotions with Younger Children. As adults with years of resolving conflict and sophisticated communication skills behind us, we sometimes fall short of communicating with a child at his or her level. Conversation itself involves cognitive (thinking) skills that develop with age. A four year-old child is not capable of communicating in the same way as a seven year-old child, or a ten year-old or a fourteen year-old or an eighteen year-old. Physical growth and development is often a lot easier to notice than is cognitive development; yet as children progress physically, they are still developing intellectual skills, moving from very concrete thinking as children to more abstract thinking and reasoning as they become young adults. In any case, we must remember to enter their world at their level if we are going to be most useful.

- **Art Work.** Providing children with an opportunity to express themselves through art is great. Very often a pre-school child with few verbal skills can let you know how he or she feels by drawing with crayons. Art work which shows heavy, dark marks may reflect anger. Art work in which things are small and tightly drawn may reflect anxiety. Either of these types of drawing can reflect fear. In any case, besides sometimes reflecting feelings, the simple act of creating can itself help relieve stress.

- **Playing Animals.** Another way to let kids relieve stress is to "play animals." You can tell them they can be any animal(s) they want. A very angry child might choose to be a lion or a tiger or a fierce dog. Making noises and/or speaking as the animal can relieve stress a child might be feeling just by virtue of keeping certain feelings inside. Giving them a character to play, in this case, an animal, who is much more "free" to express something loud or scary or aggressive can be a helpful, fun way to allow those feelings to emerge.

- **Puppet Shows & Story-Telling.** In the same vein as art work and playing animals, puppets and story-telling can be an outlet for children's emotions. One creative Grandpa I know made a set of puppets he gave names to such as Angry Alan, Sad Susie, Bashful Betty, and Fearful Freddy. As children played with these puppets, they were able to give them voices and reveal a great deal of themselves by making choices about which puppet to play with and what story to act out. Simple, oral story-telling can work in the same way. One fun way to tell stories together is to have one person start the story, and then have each person in the room take turns adding a sentence or two until the story is finished.

While I always advocate honesty, forthrightness, and clear communication, playing animals or doing art projects or playing with puppets or telling stories may facilitate discussions with young children about their emotions that aren't so very direct; in other words, it can be easier to talk with a young child about how he felt playing lion or drawing a big, black building than about how he felt when his father didn't pick him up on time yesterday. A young child might not necessarily know he's mad at his father for something he did or failed to do, but he still has his anger inside, and it needs to come out. Kids don't always know why they're upset, but expressing the upset is important nonetheless. So although you might have a very good idea what the child is upset about, an indirect expression of it, rather than a direct conversation about it, may be best for the child.

There are posters or drawings which show all kinds of faces displaying a whole range of human emotions (e.g., happy, sad, angry, depressed, shy, surprised, tearful, etc.). If you can locate or make one of these, and have it easily visible, or even show it directly to a child, this can also help start conversations.

Communicating about Emotions with Older Children. While the suggestions above can work well with older kids, you can also provide them with opportunities to talk more directly, which can relieve stress and anxiety very efficiently. You might begin by sharing, though not in an overly detailed way, some of the things you feel stressed about. Then solicit them to share some of theirs. Sharing may be the best way to encourage honest communication.

Always remember that with young people, it's easier for them if you share first. But also listen to them; they will let you know through their casual conversation what their interests are, and you can always use what they tell you as tips for organizing activities which might be productive and stress-relieving, including meals out in restaurants, fishing, cooking, woodworking, walks and more vigorous forms of exercise, sports, amusement parks, shopping trips, movies, etc. Try to hear what they reveal about themselves; demonstrate your interest in who they are by suggesting activities that might interest them.

Just spending time alone together can encourage your grandchildren to trust that you are available to listen. You might also say so directly (e.g., "I love you. If you ever feel troubled — sad, or angry, or nervous — I'm always available to listen."). Emphasizing your role as listener rather than advice-giver can actually be more supportive. If your grandchild does share his or her feelings with you and you do have advice to offer, ask in a gentle way if it is wanted before you assume that it is (e.g., "This situation with your friends sounds tough, but not impossible. Do you want some suggestions?"). You may want to highlight an experience of your own that was similar — often young people feel not only troubled, but alone in their troubles, as though no one else has ever gone through what they're going through. So you can let them know that you've "been there." In any case, be sure not to imply that it's better to take your advice than to try to resolve an issue on his or her own. Respect your grandchildren's feelings and their right to have their own problems and to find their own solutions. And, of course, be there for them when they need you.

Again, the sources of stress can differ vastly among young people, but the situation can be particularly sensitive when they are upset about things going on with their parents. For example, children sometimes feel disloyal when they are worried about their parents. Given enough support, however, they may feel able to share these concerns with grandparents. Just listening and giving the kids a "sounding board" can be enough. Respect their privacy, honor their confidences, don't pry, and do let them know you're available to listen if they want you to.

Finally, let me just say that the first lesson we want to teach our grandchildren about emotions is that it's okay to have <u>all</u> feelings, that it's just fine to feel sad or angry or lonely or upset or jealous or frightened, and that those are just as legitimate as feelings of happiness and pleasure and hopefulness. Of course it's tremendously important that we believe this to be true for ourselves — only then can we expect to be capable of teaching it to our grandchildren.

Activities

Staying Close to Grandchildren Who Live Far Away

What most of us want is to be heard — to communicate.

— DORY PREVIN

As a preface to the section on activities, I just wanted to include a few notes on staying close when you can't be with your grandchildren in person.

My little granddaughter Melanie and toddler grandson Ryan live several hundred miles from me. I have been lucky, though, because their parents have let me take care of them for a week at a time on more than one occasion.

Now, even though I've had the luxury in the past of living right next door to two of my grandsons, there's another kind of bonding altogether that takes

place when my grandchildren come and stay at our house overnight without their parents. Getting the kids ready for bed, reading them nighttime stories, learning their routines, giving them baths, waking up in the morning and having breakfast together, even going through a few of the crabby hours together have all enriched our bonding. I always feel that we're just a little closer after one of these visits.

Visiting with Your Grandchildren

Time alone for grandparents and grandchildren is very important. Given the distance, my husband and I are fortunate enough to be able to make trips or arrange for them to come to us every few months or so. In this respect, we're also lucky that the children's parents see the value of grandparenting.

Sometimes when grandparents travel to be with their grandchildren's families it's a good idea to stay at a motel rather than in the home. Being in your grandchildren's home is fun, of course, and it allows you to be a part of everything, but it's important to recognize that both grandchildren and their parents lead very active lives. If there are two or three kids coming and going, and their mother and father have lots of commitments, friends, etc., sometimes having grandparents visit only adds to the confusion.

By staying outside the home you can plan better times for them and for you during your visit. Picking up the children and taking them for an afternoon downtown or at the zoo gives parents a chance to catch a break and get some of their own chores done. Taking the kids out on a Saturday night, or even "baby sitting" them at home so the parents can have a night out for themselves is another wonderful thing to do. If your motel or hotel has a swimming pool, restaurant, or an arcade, bringing the kids there to visit for a couple of hours can also be a special treat. When everyone's back at home and you're alone again, you can catch up on your rest, have some quiet time to yourselves, and prepare for another day of active involvement with the family.

Whether visiting your grandchildren or having them visit you, I can't emphasize enough how important it is to take each grandchild somewhere individually. An hour of one-on-one attention is worth more than a whole week of confusion and chaos. Family get-togethers can be so hectic that no one actually gets to know anyone any better. And isn't that the whole point of making trips and taking the time to be together?

Grandchildren Visiting You

Taking care of babies and toddlers in your home is sometimes difficult because your house or apartment may not be set up for little ones. If your grandchildren are young, ask their parents to remind you once again how to "child-proof" your home. Avoiding dangerous accidents is ALWAYS worth whatever you have to do. Also remember that toddlers need constant attention in order to be safe. Sometimes it's easy to forget when we've been away from children, but we can remind and re-train ourselves about how to be alert. And remember, taking care of babies and toddlers is a real gift to new parents who could really use a break. So it's important to develop enough of a bond with your young grandchildren that they can visit you without having their parents present. This also gives you a chance to get to know each other better.

Plan activities to enjoy together with your grandchildren. There are lots of ideas on the following pages!

Telephone Calls & Mailings

Letting older kids call collect when they want to make contact with you is a great way to stay connected to grandchildren. With younger kids there can be a lot of fun, too. Ryan, who loves the portable phone and walks around his house while he's talking to us, always points out things he sees that he believes we can see too, since we're talking on the phone with him! Grandpa Joe has had some mixed experiences on the telephone...

Telephone calls can be somewhat frustrating the kids are so young that you're asking all the questions and the answers are always along the lines of, "Uh huh," and "uh uh." As the children get older they become more spontaneous and conversational, and it's much more entertaining. But with phone calls, unlike letters, once they're over they're over, and only the memory remains. We've had some fun keeping a small

tape recorder by the phone, or using our answering machine's ability to tape conversations. Then we get to listen to them again later. We don't keep these around a very long time, and usually end up taping over the old conversations with new ones, but it can be nice to refresh the memory a few days later, or to share a phone call one grandparent got to enjoy with the other grandparent who missed it.

As for using the mail, I have a routine, known as my "Friday Mailing."

I stock up on 5 x 7 manila envelopes, small bags of candy or treats, plenty of stickers (trying to keep on hand whichever ones are "in" with whatever age kids I'm sending to), and inexpensive gadgets, books, news articles, cartoons, etc. Every Friday I send a manila envelope with assorted goodies to each grandchild. My daughters tell me their kids watch the mail for "brown envelopes with stickers." The truth is that what's inside the envelope is less important than the fact that the children receive something specifically their own. This is one more way to let them know they're important to you.

Bonding With New Grandchildren

Anyone who has been a parent knows how much hard work it is. Grandparenting, on the other hand, is almost all pleasure. You can begin the grandparenting experience the minute you know you are going to have a grandchild. (I went out and bought a rocking chair that I used to sit in, planning and dreaming during my daughter's pregnancy.) There are also things you can do with your grandchildren very early in their lives that will bond you to them forever.

Keeping a Baby Journal

From the moment you learn you are going to become a grandparent, you can begin to grow close to your grandchild. One way to do this is to keep a journal or diary of your thoughts and feelings about this child before he or she is even born. Years later, you can share this volume, or special entries in it, with your grandchild.

Activities Surrounding the Birth

If you are fortunate enough to be able to be close to your children when a grandchild is being born, you may want to plan a family party to celebrate the birth of a new grandchild. If your family chooses, you may even share in the birth experience. If, however, distance prevents you even being close by, you can still make sure your children know you feel a part of the excitement and joy. Send cards and letters. Ask for photographs of pregnant Mom. Stay in close contact and keep up with as many details as the parents are willing to share. Be sure to take the initiative and express your interest.

Send flowers or a card to the parents at the time of the birth; try sending bright balloons for the child.

Once the child has been at home for a little while, you may want to send a large photograph of yourself to be kept in the baby's room, and/or send cassette tapes of your voice humming or singing songs or just speaking to the child as you might if you could be close by. This can allow your grandchild the opportunity to become familiar with what you look and sound like so that when you finally get a chance to meet in person, you will already be somewhat familiar.

Special Smells

When you do have the opportunity to be near a new baby in your family, hold him or her as much as you can. You might want to make sure the fragrance you wear around the child is very soft because babies can feel easily overwhelmed by strong smells, and that it's the same scent each time you're together. This applies to grandmas and grandpas alike — if you don't wear fragrance, you can think in the same ways about your soap and shampoo. The important thing to remember is that a newborn child can be exquisitely sensitive to smell — this is usually one of the ways it comes to know its mother well. The same can be true for anyone who comes into close physical contact with the child. The baby will come to recognize the way you feel and smell as well as the sound of your voice. Holding, cuddling, touching, talking, singing... all of these are special techniques for making yourself familiar to an infant.

Another thing you can do with fragrance is to put just a slight amount of whatever fragrance you wear when you're with the child onto some cotton balls, and when you send a special package or letter, include a couple of these specially scented cotton balls. Some of these can also be hung next to your picture in the nursery area if the child's parents don't object. This way your grandchild can have a visual reminder connected to a particular scent, and so enjoy both of these associations with you.

Grandpa Joe on Changing Diapers

As a man, as a father, and as a grandfather, something I never expected to have to do, and something I actively avoided for as long as I could, was one of the most important rituals of having a new child in your life... changing the diaper.

I had always feared full diapers! In today's world there are disposable diapers, baby wipes, and velcro fasteners, all of which made the chore much less worrisome in terms of fears and frustrations around sharp, awkward pins and tender new skin, none of which is to say that there aren't still things that may be a bit unpleasant about the task. But there is some amazing bonding that occurs through the act as well. On about the fifth or sixth occasion I had been called on to participate, I began to notice that the baby actually stares at you throughout the process. Very young children may focus for more uninterrupted time on the persons who change them than on anything else they encounter during a day. So there I am, changing a diaper, using the wipes again, and again, and again, trying to do my best and not fumble, and even wondering if the baby notices my ineptness. But while all this is going on, I'm being stared at, and I very quickly learn to stare back, and I think I have found a new communication with babies that I imagine no one else has ever discovered. Of course when I look at my wife or my daughter-in-law to see if I'm right, I realize they've known this part of the ritual all along.

Grandpa Joe on Sharing an Overnight with a Baby or Toddler

As "Grandpa Joe," when our young grandson came to stay overnight it was up to me to make him feel welcome and safe. We slept in the spare bedroom together. It's wonderful to be asleep in the same room where a grandchild may be in his crib. Upon waking in the morning, you find two little eyes staring at you patiently from a serious little face which, when it sees your eyes open and your body begin to stir, breaks into a big smile. It is wonderful to hear the baby talk issuing forth from this tiny creature who is ready to begin another day of perpetual motion. You feel like you have a grandchild, student, and best friend all wrapped up in this special 28-pound bundle.

These moments of intimacy build a relationship that cannot be replicated by any other. When I pick up my grandson and we head for breakfast, we're an unbeatable team.

Special Music

You can learn to hum just one or two simple melodies that will be your "signature" soothing sound for the baby. If you feel absolutely unmusical, perhaps you can recite the lyrics to a lullaby in a soft, rhythmic voice.

Today, as a grandmother myself, I can still hear in my mind and heart a melody that was hummed to me as a baby and small child, and even today these remembered sounds bring great comfort.

♫ Hush little baby ♪♪
Don't you cry... ♫

Meal Time with a Baby

Feeding is a bonding activity like no other, though it can also be extremely frustrating. A friend of ours describes his grandmother as the person to whom he had only to say he was hungry and he could make her day. There is something about providing nourishment and sustenance to our young ones that is just exhilarating. The beauty of a nursing mother, the stare of a child in a high chair watching every move as cereal is being prepared, the reflexive opening of a tiny mouth... all of these lovely images seem to black out when the spoon of food comes close to the tiny waiting face and the little aperture of a mouth slams shut.

The good thing about such moments is that the baby usually finds them funny, and not even a child can laugh with a closed mouth, so there's a great opportunity in the very next moment to get that food where it's supposed to be going.

As mothers bond with nursing infants, so, too, can a grandparent bond when bottle- or spoon-feeding a young child.

Growing With a Pre-School or School-Age Grandchild

The pre-school years are key to establishing a relationship with your grandchildren, for this is the time during which they develop real recognition, trust, and connection. Do all that is possible to spend time with your grandchildren during this phase in particular. The following activities are designed for you and your pre-school and young school-age grandchildren.

Family Book

One of the things my two daughters have done to help their children get to know their grandparents is making up a little scrap book in which children can write and draw about their grandparents.

Take a small scrapbook, even 4" x 6" will work, and paste in a photograph of Grandma. Beside it have some key phrases about Grandma: *Grandma lives on a farm.... Grandma has black hair.... Grandma's dog is named Muffin....* Do the same on the following page for Grandpa: *Grandpa is very busy working during the year.... Grandpa likes to dance.... Grandpa plays golf or cards....* This can be done with many relatives to begin to give the child a sense of the family beyond the one in the house in which he or she lives. You can include aunts and uncles and cousins. By the time my grandchildren were beginning to speak they could recognize Aunt Sue, Uncle Pat, Grandma Sharon, and Grandpa Joe. They knew who these people were as easily as they knew Mickey Mouse and Donald Duck and Santa Claus. Best of all, they began to get a sense of these relatives as members of their own special family.

Later, this book can be built upon and, as children get older, photos can be accompanied by lengthier descriptions, or even short stories about the real lives of the people in the pictures. For example, some of the things I have added to books include photographs and some text about Grandpa Joe riding horses, and a little story about how Grandpa Joe likes to play golf. Next to a photo of myself in my garden, I added some details: *This is Grandma Sharon, who likes to plant flowers, and these are some of her flowers.*

What you actually create is a kind of story book that allows the child to get to know something of the lives and personalities of his relatives.

I plan to ask my children to make me similar books about my grandchildren, a scrapbook of their activities, with text or stories to help me know them as fully as possible from far away: *This is Melanie playing with her puppies.... This is Christopher learning how to walk.... This is Matthew riding his bike.... This is Ryan going to school.... This is Cheyenne with her dolls....*

These family books can be mailed back and forth and they can be updated so that families stay close together in thought and through story.

Audio and Video Tapes

Building on the same concept as the family books is the idea of making both audio and video tapes. My grandchildren, like so many children, spend many hours in the car seat going places with their parents. It's great to have audio tapes they can listen to in the car. You can speak directly to the child or children, almost like an oral letter, telling them what's new in your life, about preparing for a special holiday, about when you slipped and fell into a puddle in the rain, about how you're feeling and what brought you a lot of pleasure recently, etc. They can do the same for you, too. Grandparents' and grandchildren's news reports can help keep everyone involved with each other.

And now that we're all so video oriented, there are may things that can be done with this medium as well. Before my grandchildren moved away, for example, I was concerned that at their tender ages of almost four and two, it would be easy for them to forget or somehow "lose" so much of the bonding we had already shared. So one of the things Joe and I did was to take the kids on a trip. Because it's highly unlikely that at these ages the kids would be able to remember anything of the trip after a little while, we put it all on video. We edited it down afterwards, added some music, and now the kids watch it as an entertainment video. My daughter says that in addition to the enjoyment the kids get from watching the tapes, these videos actually stimulate their memories of other aspects of the trip. Until the time that we can all take another trip together, the videos can help us all continue to enjoy the ones we've already taken together.

Pictures

With grandchildren children this age you can begin to send pictures back and forth through the mail, or, if you live nearby, to exchange them in person (although every child loves to get mail — it's very exciting — so even if you live close by, this is an inexpensive way to share a special kind of activity with your grandchildren). I went out and bought a children's coloring book. I color the pictures, tear them out, and send them to my toddler grandchildren. I ask them to color pictures and send them to me. This way we can keep each other's art work posted on the refrigerator, and there's a real sense of things going back and forth, of sharing.

I also buy stickers for the envelopes I use so my grandchildren who can't yet read can easily recognize the envelope as a communication for them. Now I'm starting to get envelopes back from my grandchildren and they also use stickers!

Bulletin Board

For a holiday, you can give each grandchild a bulletin board. In the corner it can say "Grandma loves you" or "Grandpa loves you" (or both), and whenever you have letters and pictures and photographs and so on that are mailed back and forth, these can be posted on the bulletin board. You can also keep in your home a bulletin board for each child, to hold all of the things that come to you in the mail from that child. If you don't live nearby or your grandchildren can't visit your house very often, you can even send each of them a photograph of the bulletin board you keep in your house for posting his or her special items. This photograph may even end up on the grandchild's bulletin board, emphasizing the ways in which you share this activity, and the joy of giving and receiving with each other.

Bedtime Story

Another activity that can keep grandparents and grandchildren close involves telling bedtime stories. If you live far away, you still don't have to miss out on this wonderful time with a child. Even if you live near by, you probably don't share this time with your grandchildren in a very regular way, so you too can follow this idea. Tell a special bedtime story to your grandchild on a cassette tape that can be mailed or brought over and left at the child's house. Every night he or she can listen to you telling this special story. Imagine the joy when you get to visit with each other, and the child can actually hear the story in person!

Once there was a little boy who lived with his mom and ..

Special Dishes

Giving a grandchild a set of personalized plastic dishes (these are usually available by mail ordering) that bear a photograph of the two of you together and/or the words "Grandma Sharon Loves You" or "Grandpa Jake Loves Sam," or any other message you choose can be yet another way to be remembered daily.

In place of a photograph, some companies can take drawings and reproduce them on plastic eating ware. You can use a drawing made by you, by your grandchild, or by the two of you together.

Music

There are so many wonderful songs and musicians, you can find many ways to enjoy music with your grandchildren.

In my work as a therapist and in my role as Grandma, I have found one musician who has added tremendously to my life and to the lives of my grandchildren — Peter Alsop. Peter is a songwriter as well as a performer. His songs are fun, easy to sing, and often carry a very special message. There are songs on his albums which deal with topics ranging from drug abuse to keeping your room clean to women's role in society to sibling rivalry, and more. Some of his titles alone should give an idea of the spirit of his music.

"I Am a Pizza" — fun sing-along

"Nobody Knows for Sure" — children and terminal illness

"My Body is No Body's Body but Mine" — sexual abuse

"My Father's Top Drawer" — sexual education

"I Wanna Be a Dog" — pure fun

"When Jesus Was a Kid" — understanding Christmas

"The Night Before Hanukkah" — celebration

I've had the opportunity to see Peter at many workshops and conferences, and he and his music are always enjoyed by both the young people and the adults present. You can look for his music in your local cassette and CD stores, or you can write to him directly for more information. He can be reached by writing to:

Peter Alsop / Box 960 / Topanga, California 90290

Helping Make Telephone Connections

When older children, teens, or adults speak to one another by phone, they are, for the most part, easily able to call up a visual image of the person with whom they are speaking. For little children who are just beginning to develop all of their cognitive faculties, this is not the case, especially, of course, if they have never met you, or have only been in your presence when they were quite young.

You might want to ask your children if they would be willing to keep a photograph of you near the telephone so that when you call and speak with your grandchild, he or she will have an opportunity to look at your picture, and in that way have a visual image of you while hearing your voice.

Magic Tricks

My husband always carries around a play thumb in his pocket. This is less gruesome than it sounds, because it brings so much delight to our grandchildren and their friends and anyone else's grandchildren who might just happen to be sitting across from us in a restaurant.

With the use of this magic prop and a tissue, Joe makes his "thumb" do little disappearing act, and kids are just thrilled by this. He doesn't come on real strong — he'll just be sitting there, doing his little tricks, and pretty soon he'll catch the kids' eyes.

He has more magic tricks — this is just the one he has with him at all times. In any case, he's become known as the Grandpa with the magic.

Any ongoing form of play that your grandchildren clearly enjoy (try it out a few times before making a real habit of it) can be a powerful way for children to identify you, remember you, and relate to you.

Games

Some grandparents will carry a deck of cards with them at all times
so that they are always ready for a game of Go Fish or Crazy 8s or
Gin Rummy with children. If you don't like cards, or don't have any
handy, all you need for a game of Hangman or Tic Tac Toe is a pencil
and a piece of paper. Most children enjoy games, and it's great to
have a few around that are age-appropriate for your grandchildren.

Most children need to win games at least part of the time to
stay interested and to feel a important sense of mastery or success at
what they do. But it's not really a good idea to always "let" your
grandchild win — losing is part of playing, so this is an aspect of
play that children need to master also. Use your judgement.

Refrigerator Art

Many grandparents receive special pictures and art from their grand-children. We display ours proudly on our refrigerator. Then we take a photograph of the refrigerator covered with kids' art, and send it to the grandchild with a thank you note for the art he or she sent us.

The principle here is a lot like the idea of the Bulletin Boards suggested earlier. Letting children see in a photograph exactly how and where you've placed the art they made especially for you is a way of deepening the connection, and of encouraging more art to be made just for you.

When new art arrives, the "old" art goes into a scrapbook. When grandchildren come to visit, they can look through their own art book as if they are visiting a gallery showing off their work.

A Fun Guessing Game

When my children were very little we used to play a game called "Guess What I'm Seeing." This has become a fun game to play with my grandchildren. One of the best things about it is that you can play it anywhere, even in the kitchen while you're making a meal, because it's an easy game to enjoy while you're doing something else.

One person says "I see something and it's green." Of course, the something has to really be within your field of vision while you're playing. The other person looks around and guesses all of the green objects he or she can see until naming the right one. With younger children, you can add all kinds of descriptive details to it so that they get more clues about what the object might be: "I see something in the corner of the room, and it's green and it's about a foot high and it's got about 50 little pieces to it...." (In this case the object would be a plant.)

This can be a good car game, but you do have to remember that you can only play the game for as long as the thing you're seeing (a particular bridge or building or structure or bit of nature or land-scape) is in view. Once you've passed it, and you can't really see it any-more, it won't work.

Paper Chains

When young children are first learning how to use scissors, one really fun activity can be cutting strips of paper to create paper chains. First let them cut strips. I have found that construction paper works best. Then they can glue or scotch tape the first strip to form a circle, and attach more strips, one at a time, to make a great paper link chain. The last time I did this with my grandchildren it probably took up about two hours of concentrated time. I didn't remember kids having that kind of attention span, but these guys were fascinated, first by the cutting, then by the taping, and the longer the chain got, the more excited they became.

Grandpa Joe has also found that the children love to receive occasional shipments every once in a while of the tractor strips from his computer paper. He saves these after printing and sends them to the children, who can make long, long chains with them.

Paper Plate Masks

A craft idea that kids of all ages seem to enjoy is making masks with paper plates and popsicle sticks. Younger kids really seem to have a lot of fun with masks, and older kids get very creative.

Glue the popsicle stick to a very thin paper plate. This can be the handle. Then let the kids make different masks they can hold in front of their faces. They love making animals and scary monsters. You can use pipe cleaners and cotton for beards or fur or whiskers, eyebrows, or mustaches. Good things to have on hand for this project include bright markers, glue, glitter, tissue paper, felt fabric scraps, and beads and feathers.

It can be a little awkward to cut the eyes and mouth (and some will want holes for their own noses to show through, too) out of the paper plate. With younger, less coordinated or less skilled kids, it's a good idea if you make these cut-outs first, before they even glue on the stick. Except with much older kids, children's scissors should be used for all the rest of the cutting.

When the masks are finished, the kids might even want to put on a little skit, play, or other type of performance.

Envelope Games

Another fun game involves saving all the envelopes you receive in a month's time. You can just keep them in an empty shoe box tucked away in a closet somewhere. You'll find they accumulate really quickly. Then, in a hobby store, buy very inexpensive stickers, which can become "pretend" stamps. If you get your collection going in about six or seven different shoe boxes, you can place them in different parts of your house and the kids can play post office. They can carry the mail around from box to box, delivering it to the grown ups and to each other, or just to another "post office" shoe box. All you have to do is get them started on this one — they'll make up endless games with it themselves.

Avocado and Potato Plants

Making plants out of avocado pits and potatoes is fun and easy. Just take the potato and put three toothpicks in its flesh so that you can suspend it over a glass of water with only half the potato below the surface of the water. In a week or two the potato will start to root in the glass, and shoots will start to grow into the air from the dry side. If you use an avocado pit, the same thing will happen, only as roots grow down into the water, leaves will start to grow up into the air. After the roots have grown you plant the pit or potato in soil in a roomy pot and water the soil frequently. Avocado pits makes lovely plants which can actually grow quite tall. Potato plants will grow in the same way.

Getting to Know Your Grandchild

It's important to remember that with very young grandchildren, the grandparents have to initiate most conversations. But most children will respond. So go ahead and get to know them!

1) Ask what your grandchild would wish for if given three wishes.
2) Talk about favorite and least favorite foods, and favorite and least favorite colors. Try to find out why the child likes/dislikes these.
3) Discuss the television show your grandchild likes the most.
4) Talk about what music he or she likes.
5) Ask about favorite things to do after school.

You don't need to ask all for these questions at once. In fact, it's probably a good idea if you don't — this could overwhelm a child, making him or her feel as though you're conducting an interrogation instead of a friendly conversation. Each of the above suggestions is for a separate conversation. If you want to link a few together, you can try to start by saying, "Let's talk about your favorite things, and what makes you like them so much." Then you can go from one topic to the next (e.g., food to color to t.v. show). But take your cues from the child, too. If he or she seems to be getting fidgety, don't press for more. If he or she is enjoying the conversation, you'll know, and you can keep going.

At a certain age, a child will want to know what your favorite things are, and compare his or her answers with yours. It's nice if you can discover that you share some favorites.

Taking a Class with Your Grandchild

Take a class with a growing grandchild. There are art classes, cooking classes, computer classes, language classes, outdoors classes, and lots more. Look in local community center or community college catalogues, or check with your grandchild's school or after-school program. Call your YMCA or Jewish Community Center. You might choose something leisurely like fishing lessons, or make it a real learning experience with reading, math, or a foreign language as the topic. Cooking classes can also be fun. For those grandparents lucky enough to live close by, or for those who get to be close by for long period of time over the summer or throughout the year, this is a great way to spend some really valuable time with a grandchild.

The Value of Money

This is something that can occur while you're doing other things together. But when you go to a restaurant, gas station, movie theater, or a store, let the children pay the money. This can make them feel important, and a real part of the activity. You can also help grandchildren pick out Mother's Day, Father's Day, holiday or birthday presents for their parents, other grandparents, or siblings. These are opportunities for them to learn that money has value, that it "doesn't grow on trees," and that certain things cost more or less than others. As they get older, children can begin to grasp these concepts more fully, and can even begin to learn about counting change, and making sure they're giving and receiving the correct amount in any monetary exchange.

Field Trips

Watch the paper for special events that you might not even consider attending alone. Sharing an environment that's new to both people can be a special experience for a grandparent and grandchild. So watch for concerts, craft fairs, art fairs, even county fairs (where kids can have an especially great time walking through the animal barn and seeing the live exhibits).

It can also be a lot of fun to team up with another set of grandparents and their grandchildren, have a big breakfast together, and all go together to the zoo, circus, kids' museum, or special event such as an ice skating show or children's concert. You can do these things with children with whom your own grand kids are already familiar, or make it an opportunity to meet some other children in a context where there is an outside activity going on; this can decrease the pressure some children feel around meeting new people, especially if they're shy or quiet or just not in the right mood.

Sleepovers

Sleeping over at a grandparents' house can be a new and exciting adventure. It can be fine just to stay in a spare bedroom or on the living room couch, of course, but it might be even more fun to sleep in a new way — outside in tents and sleeping bags, or pumping up air mattresses to set out on the living room floor or in a spare room. Some of our special sleepovers have been spent "camping" in front of the fireplace... everyone, including Grandma and Grandpa, in sleeping bags in the family room... on lawn chairs out on the deck underneath the stars... in front of the television with a special movie on in the dark....

Teaching Skills

As your grandchildren get a little bit older, one great way of spending time together is to teach some special skills, perhaps providing some training or education the child's parents don't have time to oversee, or augmenting skills they're already learning at home or school. It really helps if there are some immediate rewards so the kids can see the results of their labors. Examples include everything from running a tape recorder to learning to use certain tools such as hammers or screwdrivers. Cooking also involves "tools" we commonly refer to as appliances and gadgets (e.g., a can opener, a stove, a hand-held mixer, a sifter for dry ingredients in baking, etc.). You can teach a child how to hammer a nail into the wall in order to hang a picture, or how to make certain crafts for themselves or as gifts for others. For kitchen skills, there are plenty of children's cookbooks in which the recipes are quite simple and fun. In good weather, a child can learn the basics of gardening.

Learning and mastering such skills will help any child feel increasingly self-sufficient, and this is great for self-esteem. Teaching is also a wonderful way for grandparents to feel helpful, involved, and nurturing. Remember to be patient and to go at the child's pace. A three year-old may be able to help stir some of the ingredients while baking, but you should stay close by to help hold the bowl. A seven year-old may be ready to learn how to hammer a nail, but may not yet have the fine coordination it takes to handle a screwdriver. And, whether you're in the garage, kitchen, garden, or anywhere else, always teach safety first.

Computer Games

This past summer I was visiting my grandchild and the potential value of computer games became very clear as I realized he had learned the location of every one of the United States, as well as almost every major country and many minor ones through his computer game, "Where in the World is Carmen Sandiego?" This was amazing to see. Every night he sits down with his globe and looks for countries and makes up games about travel. He and his father have also made up games that give them some good times together. And Grandpa Joe loves getting in on all this fun!

T.V. Opportunities

It was mentioned earlier that one of the things you can talk to your grandchild about are his or her favorite television programs, but the conversation can be even more interesting if you watch the shows too, or, better still, if you can watch them together.

Watching television together can be fun and even, in some cases, educational. Special sports events such as the Olympics are great for fun and learning, but they're broadcast only once every few years. Team sports such as basketball can be exciting, *Sesame Street* is always fun, and PBS specials on nature or history are usually fun and enlightening no matter how old you are. So make some popcorn, pour some juice or sodas, and settle in together!

You might want to discuss with the child's parents what he or she is allowed to watch on television at home. Try to respect the guidelines they set.

Disc Jockey Fun

Earlier we mentioned making special audio tapes for your grandchildren. These can be customized even further with some special editing...

Children get very excited when they hear a tape with a commercial song on it that is then followed by a 'disc jockey' narration by Grandpa or Grandma saying hi to them, using their names, or inviting them to sing along to the next song. There are also many accompaniment tapes of children's songs or religious songs which can also be used — if you can carry a tune, you may want to sing along with one of these, and then record that for your grandchild.

If your grandchild shows a particular interest in music, some special gifts can be a cassette player or a kids' microphone and recording unit. Who knows what talent this may bring forward!

Newspapers and Magazines

Watch for special newspaper or magazine articles or photographs you think might be of interest to your grandchild, who may not see a paper on a daily basis. You can also cut out special cartoons, or anything a child might be able to read on his or her own, and send these through the mail to let the child know he or she is special to you, and in your thoughts.

Another great gift for a grandchild can be a magazine subscription. This feels very grown-up to most kids, and gives them a special piece of mail to look forward to on a regular basis. There are lots of kids' magazines to choose from.

Go Fly a Kite

Every grandparent should fly a kite with a grandchild. Just get the most simple type of kite, and pick a day with a lot of wind. Let your grandchild feel in charge by giving him or her the string to hold.

Stocking Up: Inexpensive Fun When Grandchildren Come to Visit

When you know your grandchildren are coming to visit, you can begin preparations ahead of time by gathering materials you can use for fun during their stay. This takes no money, very little effort, and can provide you with hours of arts and crafts fun when they arrive.

Cardboard milk cartons (washed and dried), big and little cardboard boxes, cereal boxes, etc. are great for building structures, to draw on, or to hold things.

Old toilet paper and paper towel tubes make great telescopes or binoculars, indoor bowling pins, tunnels for small trains or race cars, etc.

Clean, used aluminum foil can be used for wrapping packages or gifts, making masks, or jazzing up any other toys or structures the kids make.

Egg cartons can be used for holding paints while painting, storing beads or screws or small parts of games and toys, or for planting seeds.

Old mail catalogues and magazines are great to cut up for collages or cards or even original "newspapers" or "magazines" that kids can make themselves around a specific theme such as sports, animals, flowers, or any topic which interests them.

Get out the supplies and have fun!

Washing the Car

Grandchildren of all ages enjoy helping wash a car as long as the activity is not made to be too strenuous, and you're not too much of a perfectionist. Soapy water, a sponge, and a hose can be a recipe for tons of giggles and joy, especially if it's a nice warm day and your grandchild can alternate playing with the water and actually helping out. When you're all done everyone can get cleaned up and take a ride in the nice clean car to get a snack or meal (being careful, of course, to keep the car clean!).

Pee Wee Golf

Slightly older children can have a great time playing miniature golf. Not all cities have these "courses," but many suburbs do. It's important to remember here that this is a game for fun, and the goal in a game of miniature golf with a grandchild is not to do it exactly right or to make par, but to have fun. Funny things can happen at a miniature golf course — relax and have a good time.

Staying Close
with Older Grandchildren

The years go by swiftly. Soon those little babies become children, and before long, young men and women. As our grandchildren grow, they will be changing, and as they change, they are our wonderful link to a growing, changing world. If we learn from them, we have a better chance of staying young. It's important to stay bonded to our grandchildren as they get older — these may be the years in our lives when we need each other the most.

Vacations

Nothing creates intimacy like being together on a vacation. You can plan some wonderful times by taking trips together with your grandchildren. There are many travel agencies and companies that plan special trips for grandparents and grandchildren. (One I know of is RFD Travel Corporation, 5201 Johnson Drive, Mission, KS 66205. Phone #: 1-800-365-5359. In Kansas City, call 722-2333.)

And though some people consider trips or visits to occur over long periods of time, lasting one to three weeks or more, weekends, long holidays, and even overnights can be just as special.

As ever, hobbies such as fishing, boating, camping, reading, and hiking can be part of these vacation times. But along with all the planned activity come the really special moments — talking, laughing, sharing — which can facilitate the transition from what might previously have been a less close relationship to a deeper, more real relationship of new closeness, honesty, and value. For those of you who are fortunate enough to be close with your grandchildren to begin with, these times together continue to enrich the relationship in an ongoing way.

Camping

Grandparents who have experience starting fires, cooking outside, crawling into sleeping bags, and counting stars have a lot to share with their maturing grandchildren. Grandchildren who have been scouts or other young campers also have much to share with grandparents.

As the day progresses from pancakes outside to daily hikes and explorations, and ends with the roaring campfire and s'mores, intimacy, trust, laughter, and closeness are natural by-products.

A simple tent with sleeping bags provides one type of camping. Actual adventure trips planned by travel agents who know where to look for grandparent-grandchild vacations are another way to get outdoors together (river rafting trips, dude ranches... there are many of these throughout the West).

Physical Fitness

In his book, *Grandparent Power*, Arthur Kornhaber states that 71% of the 9 million children between the ages of 6-17 years have failed to meet the fitness standards set by the Amateur Athletic Association (Kornhaber, A. *Grandparent Power*. New York: Crown Publishers, 1994, p. 90).

Physical activity is a wonderful way for grandchildren and grandparents to spend time together. We live in an area with many grandparents as neighbors. It's wonderful to see people in their 50s, 60s, 70s, and yes, even 80s walking, swimming, doing aerobics, dancing, and playing tennis or golf. My own aerobics instructor is 83 years old!

Everyone, young and old, can benefit from turning off the television, putting on exercise clothes, and getting out together. In addition to the physical benefits are the spiritual and emotional ones. It's pretty hard to exercise and hike outdoors without getting some appreciation of the sky, land, and surrounding areas. If your own immediate neighborhood isn't the best for this, head for a park, a lake, or some new territory. Seeking out the special place can be part of the fun.

Great conversations can occur during these times of peaceful, yet active adventure. Some of my closest moments with my own children have been spent on walks. As my grandchildren grow, it's great to start this same tradition with them.

Going to the Movies & Watching Videos

A good way to stay up-to-date with maturing grandchildren is to go to movies together. The popcorn and drinks are only part of the fun. Afterwards you can talk about what you saw, and learn a great deal about each other. Be sure to maximize opportunities for discussion with your grandchildren. Because they're so stimulating, and almost every viewer is interested in a different aspect, movies can often start discussions that might never come about any other way.

You can achieve the same closeness through renting videos together, too.

T-Shirts

Another fun activity for older children is designing and "making" their own t-shirts.

Buy new, plain white t-shirts. These are usually sold individually or in three-packs. You can get a set of non-toxic markers, glitter paints, or any number of progressively elaborate supplies at an art store, and let your grandchild create a personalized design on his or her own shirt. You can help, or make your own at the same time. Whether you work together on one shirt or each make your own, create a design that reflects an interest or talent, one which speaks to the area where you or they live (a sea shell, a pine tree, a cactus, etc.), a favorite animal, your house, the child's house, etc. The child's shirt will always be specifically his or hers, and so, all the more special. These t-shirts can be designed as gifts for other family members, too.

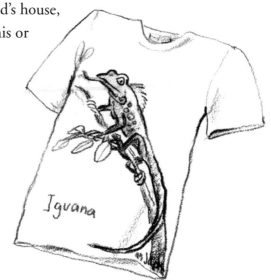

Garage & Yard Sales

Let older children have a garage sale. You can go through your home and find all kinds of unused or unwanted items. Tell your grandchildren they can make and distribute flyers in the neighborhood advertising a "yard sale" or "garage sale." Give the kids a jar or shoe box full of change, and set them up outside with a sale sign. Let them know they can keep the proceeds of whatever they sell.

Slumber Parties

Some of my happiest memories of being a teenager are of going to stay overnight with my grandmother, and bringing along one or two girlfriends. My parents and grandparents knew that teenagers need their peers. At the same time, staying bonded with my grandmother was also important. She allowed me to do both.

When we were at her house, Grandma Olson taught me and my friends such varied skills as how to make doughnuts, how to bowl, and how to care for green plants. She never fussed when we would laugh and giggle way into the night, and we all looked forward to her stories over pancakes in the morning.

It can be wonderful to let your grandchildren know that you accept and enjoy them and their friends — this is very affirming during adolescence, a complex time during which so many young people feel anything but accepted. Often times, adolescents feel as thought they aren't even sure "who" they are — embracing them together with their friends, and letting them know that they continue to have a home away from home in your house, can be comforting, reassuring, and very special indeed.

Shopping

Whether looking for clothes, jewelry, sports equipment, or books, a shopping trip between a grandchild and a grandparent can be a really special time. Include a meal at the beginning, middle, or end, and you have one more memory together.

Teaching & Learning New Skills and Hobbies

As mentioned in the first section of this book on the Many Roles of Grandparents, teaching and learning both can be wonderful ways to share together with your grandchildren. With older children, roles can reverse so that the grandparents are the students and the young people the teachers. Acknowledging that they have something to teach you is a special way of loving these young people in your life, of letting them receive your love, and love you back.

While grandparents may be able to share their skills with grandchildren in wood working, sewing, cooking, painting, art, sports, the stock market, photography, dancing, piano, car maintenance, and countless other areas, grandchildren can share their skills too, in computers, dance, sports, music, art, games, and much more.

Grandpa Carl tells about wonderful meetings between grandparent and grandchild around the computer. When they're young, children want to learn, and grandparents can teach. But later, the children move ahead in their own skills, and can often teach us. Usually, younger folks are more skilled at current computer technologies than are their grandparents. Computers can be so much fun, though, and can really facilitate communication between family members. Even without the advantages of online communication programs for sending "mail" back and forth, special programs and data bases can be designed to track family events; family newsletters can be produced, and all family members with access to personal computers, whether at home, at school, or at work can participate in producing such documents.

Grandpa John is a boatman. He is able to bring his grandchildren special knowledge of boating skills, of how to prepare the boat for an outing, set sail, and put it to rest afterwards. One of his granddaughters is an excellent cook already, and she's helped Grandpa John learn some new recipes. This really helps since John is a widower and lives alone now. Another grandson is still in high school, but he's an avid tennis player and has gotten his grandfather interested enough in the sport that he watches all the Grand Slam events, and knows the rules!

Grandma Rachel is a musician. She helps her grandchildren learn to sing and dance. She teaches them about music and about how to enjoy different types of music, different instruments or instrumental combinations. They teach her about popular music and new dance trends.

State Capitals

A fun game with older children is to list all the states with all of their capitals. Write out the states' names on individual index cards — on the other side of the cards, write each state's capital. Deal out the cards or choose from a pile — whichever side of the card is face up, the player has to guess what's on the other side.

Young Adults

As your grandchildren become young adults themselves, you can continue to deepen your relationships with them. You can continue to visit and travel together, but you probably don't need to come up with as many "planned" activities for keeping busy. And now that they're older, you can really begin to exchange ideas and intimacies on a whole new level.

Only two additional roles for grandparents come immediately to mind when considering grandchildren who are already at the brink of adulthood: that of mentor, and financial advisor.

Mentoring

Sharing around skills and hobbies has already been discussed. When a young person is at an age where he or she might be considering career options or choosing how to live as an adult within a community, large or small, grandparents once again have much to offer.

For example, Grandpa Vern believes in public service. He can share with his grandchildren the importance of making a contribution to one's community, of standing up for your beliefs, of running for office, of volunteering your time.

Grandma Jessie is a doctor. She tells her grandchildren of her commitment to medicine and to people. They can visit her office or a hospital with her, and learn about the environments where science and caretaking meet.

Grandpa Lawrence takes his adult grandchildren into the family-run business during the summer months. He wants each grandchild to learn something about the business he built from scratch. Any grandchild who shows interest can spend even more time learning the details — if enough interest is demonstrated, the grand-child is invited to join the business.

Finances

Grandparents who may seem "out of touch" in some ways to young people may nonetheless have an air of financial security about them. Young adults who sometimes scoff at the ideas and styles of grandparents have to acknowledge that these older people often have homes to live in, provide grandchildren with gifts, pay their own bills, take care of themselves and others, maintain their cars, etc. In other words, it would seem that somewhere along the way, these folks did something right, and managed to plan for their own futures!

If grandchildren can respect this about their grandparents, then perhaps they can learn a thing or two from them about handling money. Stocks and bonds may be given directly to grandchildren as gifts, but even if that's not possible, financial advice can be given. This can be a powerful point of connection because one way or another, money affects everyone's life.

Adult grandchildren may be fortunate enough to have their own finances and may be making investments on their own, which they can also teach you about.

In many families discussions of money are taboo. If you and your grandchildren do decide to share confidences about these matters, do so honestly — talk about your financial misfortunes or hardships as well as your successes. We can all learn from each other's mistakes as well as achievements.

A Final Idea:
The Family History Project

When I had my first child, I felt a new bond with my own mother that came from sharing the experience of being a parent. Similarly, when I became a grandmother, I began to think of my own grandparents in new ways. It has always struck me with some sense of sorrow that my grandchildren will never know my parents, let alone my grandparents, all of whom mattered so much to me. We're all part of the same family, but today I am the only living link between the past and the present. I wanted to be able to give my children's children some sense of their legacy that isn't about objects or material goods handed down through generations, but, rather, a way of knowing their relatives, including those whom they will never get a chance to meet. Sharing details, memories, and stories is one way to do this.

If you give your grandchildren some of their past, they can carry this forward into the future....

Human beings have been telling each other stories for as long as we've had language; the impulse to recount things that have happened (or, in the case of fiction, that might have happened) is a part of our nature. And today's children grow up with stories in many forms — in our culture these might include nursery rhymes, fairy tales, story books, Bible stories, movies, television, literature, biographies, and even articles about favorite musicians, actors, and pop culture figures. Through exposure to all of these narratives, young people develop almost without realizing it an appetite for characters and plots — two elements of good stories. Well, every family has characters and plots, too; every family has its stories, full of details and emotions, full of life.

By sharing your memories, you can share your family's stories with your grandchildren. You can give them a look into the past, and a sense of legacy. You can give them knowledge about where their family has been, and how its members got to the places they are today. If you give your grandchildren some of their past, you're giving a part of themselves they can carry forward into the future.

For many relatives, you may not have stories, just details or scattered information. This is fine, too. Include what you can; you will still be adding to your grandchild's sense of family history.

For those of you whose families may have welcomed adopted or step-children into your lives and hearts, this Family History can be just as special and wonderful for them by providing a real sense of "membership" in the family they have joined.

Include what you can and you will be adding to your grandchild's sense of family history.

INSTRUCTIONS

Because each person's family is unique, every family tree is going to look different. All families experience deaths; some also experience divorces. Either of these circumstances can lead to new marriages, and perhaps new children. Some children have one set of parents, others also have step-parents, and still others may have single parents. There might be step- or half-siblings. There might be two fathers or mothers instead of a father and a mother. There might be one grand-father or six grandparents. A family could have one grandchild or fif-teen — you get the idea.

In any case, you will be putting together a booklet that tells the story of the branches on your unique family tree. You will want to tailor the sections and pages in whatever way is appropriate. If you have more than one grandchild, you will probably want to make sep-arate copies of the whole package for each of your grandchildren, changing only the opening letter and final page for each one (you will want to make these specific to each grandchild who will be receiving a copy).

The following pages are suggestions for elements to include in your Family History Project. Again, you will want to pick and choose the elements that feel right for your family's story. We hope you'll be as creative as you can and, include not just words but pho-tographs, or perhaps even copies of significant letters or momentos. You can type or word process or write the text of your family history by hand. If you do include photographs, you'll want to use paper that's heavy enough to "hold" the photograph over time. You may want to use colored paper, or plain white paper. Just be sure that

Every family tree is unique.... Tailor the sections and pages in your Family History to fit your unique family.

whatever paper you use allows the ink or type to be read easily. When you're through, you may want to take the pages to a local copy or desktop publishing service and have them spiral-bound, or you might use a hole-puncher and some bright yarn or ribbon and "sew" your pages together. You can also use staples. Whatever method you choose, the idea is to create a collection or words and pictures that is full of life, and that will last over time.

* * *

Begin with a Letter

First, we suggest you begin with a kind of opening letter to your grandchild. You can follow our format or write one of your own. This letter is a way to let the child know why you want to make this special gift to him or her, and what it means to you to be able to share the family in this special way.

You can make copies of your Family History for each of your grandchildren....

Date: _____

To My Grandchild _____ :

This Family History is a gift from me to you.

I hold in my mind and heart all of the memories that I consider treasures. People who were with me at the time may remember things differently than I do. In some cases, I'm the only one alive who remembers these things at all. In any case, I want to share some of my treasured memories with you — details and images and stories and thoughts and feelings about people in our family.

These pages will let you know some things about our family's history — good times and painful times and laughing times and sad times and utterly joyous times, like the day you came to join us. Together, these pages tell a story about people who loved, who struggled, who gained some things, and who lost some things. You already know some of these people; some of them are long since gone and you will never get to meet them in person. But I hope you can come to know them at least a little bit through these pages.

One thing is certain: these pages tell at least some of *our* story — yours and mine and all our relatives'. It's a story that you're a very big part of, now, tomorrow, and always.

I love you with all my heart.

(your signature)

[put a photo here]

Create a Family Tree

Next, you can include a family tree. For this you may want to draw a tree, and write in the names on different branches, or you may want to cut out and paste in or have copied a photograph of a tree from a magazine; if you choose to use a photograph of a tree, you will want then to paste the family members' names you have written or typed on to the picture.

Again, every family's tree is unique. How many "branches" there are will vary from family to family. You will want to go as far back as you can with the knowledge that you have. For example, you may know your own great-grandparents' names, but not know much else about them. Include their names in the family tree even if you won't be devoting any pages of recollections and stories about them. Remember, though, that on the family tree, you are a grandparent, and the relatives should all be identified in terms of who they are to the grandchild who will be receiving the Family History. In other words, your name should be on one of the grandparent branches, and your grandchild's name should be on one of the children's branches.

Choose as many branches as are appropriate for your family's tree:

Great-Grandmother(s)	Mother(s)	Cousin(s)
Great-Grandfather(s)	Father(s)	Sibling(s)
Grandmother(s)	Step-Mother(s)	Step-Sibling(s)
Grandfather(s)	Step-Father(s)	Half-Sibling(s)
Grand Aunt(s)	Aunt(s)	Children
Grand Uncles(s)	Uncle(s)	

Remember to identify these people in terms of who they are in relation to your grandchild, and not you. In other words, your name will be on a grandparent's branch of the tree; your grandchild's name will be on one of the lowest branches of the tree.

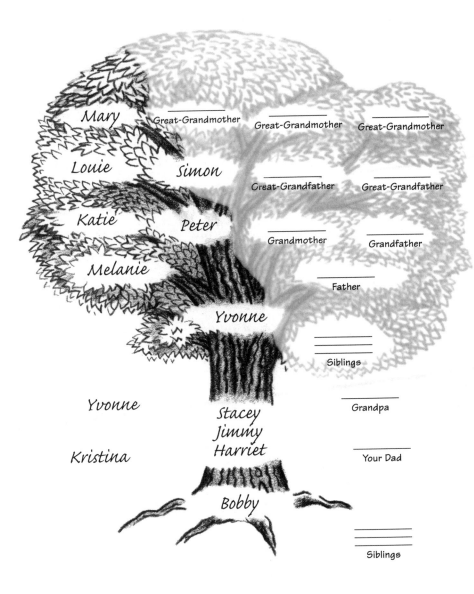

Mary

Great-Grandmother

_____ Great-Grandmother

_____ Great-Grandmother

Louie

Simon

_____ Great-Grandfather

_____ Great-Grandfather

Katie

Peter

_____ Grandmother

_____ Grandfather

Melanie

Yvonne

_____ Father

_____ _____ Siblings

Yvonne

Stacey
Jimmy
Harriet

_____ Grandpa

Kristina

_____ Your Dad

Bobby

_____ _____ Siblings

Details, Memories, and Stories

After you have finished the family tree, you can start making pages for each relative. This is the part of the project that will take the most time. Go as slowly as you like — you may want to spread the "work" out over a period of weeks or even months. This should be fun!

Use as many pages as you need for each "branch" or family member. Include facts such as name, birthday, age at time of death, and spouse's or partner's name and children's names if appropriate. You might also want to note the names of this person's siblings. For those relatives about whom you know or remember very little, this information, or some portion of this information, may be all that fills his or her page. For others, you may have lots more to share. The following is a list of suggested items to include about each relative. They are only suggestions. Feel free to use as many or as few of these ideas as you wish, or use ideas of your own:

✓ a photograph (or a physical description in your own words)

✓ this person's favorite interests or hobbies

✓ birthdate

✓ names & descriptions of any pets

✓ age at time of death (if appropriate)

✓ funny or interesting details you remember or have heard from others

✓ a favorite memory you have of this person

✓ a favorite story you know about this person

For some relatives, you may have only a few factual details to share; for others you may have a long story you wish to tell. Some pages will be very brief; others will have much more to say. Just as every family's tree is unique, this is *your* Family History Project. It will be unique to you. If you had a sister who was putting a project together for her grandchildren, her pages might end up looking completely different from yours. This is okay. This is even wonderful. One of the most amazing things about the Family History Project is that it's creative and special because *you* make it.

These pages will be mostly writing, but you may want to draw or design on computer some sort of decorative border. Whenever possible, include photographs, or copies of photographs, maybe just one or two per relative, that really capture his or her spirit or character.

If you have a story or stories you might want to tell about a particular relative, it may be very brief, or a little longer. Of course, this is up to you. You can focus on one special memory or story you know about this person, or share lots of deatails, or do both. Is there a story about this person's life that stands out? Is there a particular story about this person's life that you just know he or she would tell? Was there anything especially tragic or especially heroic about this person? Did he or she have particular pains or struggles to overcome? What do you remember most about him or her? What did you like the most about him or her? What did you like the least?

Don't be afraid to give the full picture — that is, you don't have to tell *only* the good things. Your family members may have

> *The amount of information you give will vary.... You won't have stories about every relative.*

good and bad qualities; they may be strong in some ways but weak in others. Just tell the truth as best you can.

No matter how much information you have to include, remember as you compile this family history for your grandchild that doing so is an act of love, for the child, and for the family that the two of your share. That love will surely shine through these pages.

You will probably end up with several different kinds of pages. Here are a few examples:

The Family History is creative and special because you make it....

[put a photo here]

Your Great-Grandfather Louie.

Born 3-20-1899.

Died 12-2-75.

Very handsome, even though he got a little fat later in life...
What I remember most about your great-grandfather, my father,
is that he always passed around kisses the minute he walked in
the door -- first my mother, then me, and then Freddy, our old
basset hound! If he was in a bad mood, though, none of us got
attention right away except Freddy. On Sundays, he sang opera
arias around the house!

[put a photo here]

*You may
not know
very much
about each
relative you
include....*

Uncle Jim.

Your father's brother.

Born 12-20-50.

Died 8-13-70.

Killed in Viet Nam.

Your father's side of the family so I don't know much, but from this picture he looks very handsome. Your father says Jim had been very smart in school, and had hopes of becoming a doctor when he returned from Viet Nam.

[put a photo here]

Great Uncle Troy.

Born on 9-12-23.

Worked in a bank.

Loved to build furniture as a hobby. Lives in upstate New York. Married to Aunt Celeste. Now retired.

Great Aunt Celeste.

Born on 7-7-30.

Housewife.

Mother of five! Makes the best apple cakes in the county.

You may want to combine a married couple in the family on the same page....

*You may
have more to
say about
those very
close to you:*

Your mother.

Born 5-12-55.

Graduated college with honors...

This is a photograph of your mother and me that your grand-father took when we were on vacation at the Jersey shore. In this picture, your mother is younger than you are now, and I'm pregnant with your Aunt Kate. When they were little, your mother and her sister fought all the time, and they hated sharing a room but we couldn't afford a bigger apartment. They fought about clothes and music and boys and television programs and about who made more noise eating an apple in bed and sometimes I'm just so amazed they finally turned out to be such good friends!

[put a
photo here]

Your Great-Aunt Louise.

Born 10-7-39. Died 4-21-54.

Beautiful red hair — better
than in this picture... I wish you
could have known my sister
Louise. She died of leukemia when she was just 15, and I have
missed her every day of my life since then. Louise could make
anyone laugh. In fact, she was the ONLY one who could make our
father laugh. She told the best stories — she acted out all the
parts and made everything come alive. So even if she'd been pun-
ished at school for laughing or talking in class, which happened
all the time and only didn't matter so much because Louise was
so smart and got straight As anyway, she never got in trouble at
home, even when her French teacher, Madame Lalique, was walking up the aisle where Louise sat, and slapped her eraser on
Louise's desk because Louise couldn't stop laughing and was making Madame Lalique so furious, only when she slapped the eraser
down on Louise's desk, chalk dust flew all over Mme Lalique's
new black blouse! When she told the story at home that night,
she walked all around the dinner table like she was Madame
Lalique, slapping down a dry sponge she slipped into the flour
cannister and telling all of us to stop giggling or we were going to
have to conjugate 20 new verbs, and she was slapping the sponge
down on the table and all of us were covered in flour, even Dad,
and he was laughing hardest of all....

Finishing the Project

There can never be a real "conclusion" to a family history because your family continues to live through the child or children who will receive your book(s). So your final entry in the family history will probably be the page(s) devoted to the grandchild to whom you are giving the book. If you are making several copies for several grandchildren, make sure the book that goes to each grandchild concludes with him or her. Share some of your favorite memories of your grandchild, and try to include a photograph of the two of you together. Offer some loving final words about what it means to you to have this child be a part of your family, and how proud and grateful you are to have the opportunity to be a part of his or hers.

In addition to telling you about the family, I want to tell you about myself and many of my thoughts and feelings.

Over the years, the things that have made me happiest are:

My favorite hobbies and pastimes have been:

I've been afraid of or worried about:

My plans and dreams are:

One of my greatest values and treasures has been coming to know you.

[put a photo here]

You are one of my very favorite branches on our family tree.

I remember the day I first got to meet you...

Some of the things about you that I love the most include...

My favorite story to tell about you is...

Finally, wherever you go, and whatever you do, I want you to remember that you are part of a very special family and that you are very loved. You will always be a part of my heart.

Love,

[sign your name here]

Dear Reader,

This book has been a love-task. I've wanted to write about the grandparenting experience for some time. It's been interesting and gratifying that so many people have become involved. Some people sent me stories and anecdotes and others shared activities with me. This book developed as a result.

Two additional projects will be forthcoming. One will be a newsletter for grandparents, and the other will be a sequel to *Grandparenting*.

If you have stories, helpful hints, or activities to share, please send them to me and they will be considered for the next book. You can send them to:

Sharon Wegscheider-Cruse
2561 Legend Drive
Las Vegas, Nevada 89134

To receive a free copy of the premiere issue of the Grandparenting newsletter, call 1-800-547-9982 or write to: Grandparenting, P.O. Box 60519, Palo Alto, CA 94306

As I close and say good-bye, I'd like to introduce you to my inspirations: Matthew, Melanie, Christopher, Ryan & Cheyenne.

Resources for Grandparents

ORGANIZATIONS

The following listings are by no means exhaustive. Look for local chapters of organizations and other resources in your area. In some instances, you may want to contact groups in other areas to see whether they know of groups in your region, or you may want to find out about starting a group if one doesn't already exist.

Travel

RFD Travel Corporation
5201 Johnson Drive
Mission, KS 66205
(1-800) 365-5359

Elder Hostels
75 Federal Street
Boston, MA 02110-1941

Grandtravel
6900 Wisconsin Avenue, Suite 706
Chevy Chase, MD 20815
1-301-986-0790

Grand Generations
835 West Belden Avenue
Chicago, IL 60614
1-312-929-7200

Legal Rights & Advocacy

GRAMPS (Grandparents' Rights Advocay Group)
Pat & Jack Slorah
1225 North Florida Avenue
Tarpon Springs, FL 34689

Grandchildren's Rights to Grandparents
237 S. Catherine
La Grange, IL 60525-2313

Grandparents Against Immorality and Neglect
Betty Parbs
720 Kingston Place
Shreveport, LA 71108

Grandparents Care
Marty Smith
344 S. Columbine Circle
Englewood, CO 80110

Grandparents'-Children's Rights of Missouri
Ann Conkwright
424 E. Stanford
Springfield, MO 65807

Grandparents'-Children's Rights
Lee & Lucille Sumpter
5728 Bayonne Avenue
Haslett, MI 48840

Grandparents Inc. of Central New Jersey
Alice Everett-Abner
P.O. Box 244
Piscataway, NJ 08854-0244

Grandparents' Rights Organizations
555 S. Woodward Avenue, #600
Birmingham, MI 48009
(810) 646-7191

Grandparents of Pennsylvania
R.R. 1
East Brady, PA 16028

Grandparents Reaching Out
141 Glensummer Road
Holbrook, NY 11741

Grandparents' United for Children's Rights
Ethel Dunn
137 Larkin Street
Madison, MI 53705

Grandparents Who Care
Doriane Miller, M.D. & Sue Tropin, R.N.
P.O. Box 245
San Francisco, CA 94124

Maryland Grandparents for Children's Rights
Linda Kelley, Director
7811 Flint Hill Road
Owings, MD 20736

Orphaned Grandparents Association of Edmonton
The Family Centre
9912 106th Street, 3rd Floor
Edmonton, Alberta, CN T5K 1C5

Scarsdale Family Counseling Center
Edith Engel & Marjorie Slavin
405 Harwood Building
Scarsdale, NY 10583

For Grandparents Who Are Primary Caregivers

AARP (American Association of Retired Persons)
Grandparent Information Center
601 E. Street N.W.
Washington, D.C. 20049
(202) 434-2277

ROCKING (Raising Our Children's Kids)
Box 96
Niles, MI 49120
(616) 683-2058

Grandparents Raising Grandchildren, Inc.
P.O. Box 104
Colleyville, TX 76034

Grandparents as Parents
1150 East 4th Street, Ste. #221
Long Beach, CA 90802

Second Time Around Parents
100 W. Front Street
Media, PA 91063

Support for Families & Grandparents

Parents, Family, Friends of Lesbians and Gays (PFLAG)
1101 14th Street N.W., Ste. #1030
Washington, D.C. 20005
(202) 638-4200
Grandparents' Support

NEWSLETTERS

These are wonderful newsletters for grandparents containing wondeful bits of information and ideas.

Grandparents Little Dividends
P.O. Box 11143
Shawnee, KS 66207
(913) 642-8296

Grandparents' Journal
Elinor Nuxoll
1419 East Marietta Avenue
Spokane, WA 99207-5026

Creative Grandparenting Newsletter
Creative Grandparenting, Inc.
609 Blackgate Road
Wilmington, DE 09803

BOOKS ABOUT GRANDPARENTING

Again, the list below is in no way exhaustive. Ask your local bookseller or librarian for other suggestions. If these books are not in stock, perhaps they can be special ordered.

Cherlin, Andrew J. & Furstenberg, Frank. *New America Grandparent: A Place in the Family, a Life Apart.* Basic Books. 1986.

Kornhaber, Arthur, M.D., & Woodward, Kennethy L. *Grandparents-Grandchildren: The Vital Connection.* Transaction Publishers. 1984.

Le Shan, Eda. *Grandparents: A Special Kind of Love.* Macmillan. 1984.

McBride, Mary. *Grandma Knows Best But No One Ever Listens.* Meadowbrook Press. 1987.

Wyse, Lois. *Grandmother's Treasures.* Crown Publishers, 1993.

Wyse, Lois. *Funny, You Don't Look Like a Grandmother.* Crown Publishers. 1988.

About the Author

Sharon Wegscheider-Cruse is the mother of three children and grandmother of five children. She is a professional psychotherapist with over twenty-five years' experience working with individuals and families. She has done ground-breaking work in the field of addictions and has advanced the family reconstruction technique to work with a broad spectrum of addictions and compulsive behaviors. Sharon is also the author of thirteen books, with additional titles forthcoming.